CHANNEL FOUR *Garden Club*

CHANNEL FOUR
Garden Club

ARTHUR TAYLOR

WITH AN INTRODUCTION BY
ROY LANCASTER

SIDGWICK & JACKSON

LONDON

First published 1993 by Sidgwick & Jackson Limited

a division of Pan Macmillan Publishers Limited
Cavaye Place London SW10 9PG
and Basingstoke

Associated companies throughout the world

ISBN 0 283 06153 7

1 3 5 7 9 8 6 4 2

A CIP catalogue record for this is available from
the British Library

Colour Reproduction by Aylesbury Studios, Bromley, Kent
Photoset by Parker Typesetting Service, Leicester
Printed by BPCC Hazell Books, Aylesbury, Bucks
Member of BPCC Ltd.

Contents

Introduction

When Derek Clark, then Director of Programmes at HTV (West) in Bristol, asked me to help launch a new gardening series for Channel Four I was, to put it mildly, surprised. It was the autumn of 1990 and Derek had travelled to my home in Hampshire to talk things over. The more he talked the less it sounded like my kind of programme. Don't misunderstand me; what Derek described sounded to be an ideal programme for gardeners but the frequent mention of fruit and veg, demonstrations and practical tips suggested a role for one of your all-round gardeners rather than a specialist in hardy ornamentals like me. Even when Derek told me that Channel Four's Sue Shephard had suggested he approach me, I still could not understand why.

What I hadn't appreciated was that *Garden Club,* as it was soon to be known, intended using three presenters, not one, which would allow for a broad mix of specialist interests and skills. At the end of the day I was interested enough to agree to a get-together in Bath where Derek would introduce me to producer Adrian Brenard, reporter Rebecca Pow and researcher Jo Readman, all of whom were excited about and raring to start on the new series. Exposed to their collective enthusiasm and imagination I quickly succumbed and thus began one of the most satisfying and enjoyable chapters in my working life.

Arthur Taylor in his excellent preface has described how the series is made as well as its intent. Let me therefore offer a few personal observations on its apparent success.

Once Matthew Biggs joined us as the third presenter we were all set to go. From the start we have worked as a team, presenters, production staff and crew, which has given the series a sense of unity and continuity. Not only has it been educational for us, it's also been fun and the evenings we have spent in hotels all over Britain have invariably been occupied with recounting the day's filming and the amusing things that have happened to us on our way to the gardens.

We gardeners are a funny breed, a strange mixture like a Chinese allotment. Some of us are extroverts, ever willing to show off our gardens and in particular our achievements whilst others are more private, quieter people hiding our lights under the proverbial bushel.

There are the fruit and veg fanatics whose allotments are all that matters in life, and the flower freaks who think dahlias, chrysanths and roses are the ultimate. Somewhere in between are tree and shrub nuts, bedding plant buffs, alpine enthusiasts and lawn and pond fans. We have filmed all of these on our travels and without exception they have been a pleasure to meet and work with. Their gardens have been full of surprises like the council house in Southampton whose awkwardly shaped small plot was so full of rare and unusual plants that it would have put many a botanic garden to shame.

Small gardens made by amateurs have been our mainstay on *Garden Club* and yet we have seen examples of design flair, cultivation techniques and botanical expertise that many a professional would have envied. Dedication, imagination, patience, inventiveness and hard work are qualities we have found in good measure in the gardeners we have met and it has been a privilege to share a few hours with each of them.

Almost as important to the series' success and the team's wellbeing has been the generosity shown to us by the gardeners' wives many of them gardeners themselves. The number and variety of sandwiches, buns, scones and cakes we have enjoyed would have sent Billy Bunter into ecstasies and could be the subject of a companion *Garden Club* publication. When not munching pastries and drinking tea we have discussed and demonstrated a host of tips and equipment, pruned our way through thickets of shrubs, damned almost every pest and disease in the book, planted a paradise of flowers and veg, and enthused over an army of ornamental plants old and new.

Now it all comes to life again in the *Garden Club Book* which the team is proud to be associated with. Arthur Taylor, no mean gardener himself and with an enviable record as a producer of gardening programmes, has succeeded in distilling here the essence of *Garden Club*'s success. Reading it brings back happy memories of fine gardens, busy plots and lovely people, characters all.

Derek Clark's enthusiasm wasn't so surprising after all.

ROY LANCASTER

Preface

Gardening programmes can make marvellous and successful television – there is no doubt about that. If the formula is right, then a large, loyal and enthusiastic audience will build up, the presenters will become, first, familiar faces and later, household names. The viewing figures for the series will eventually lodge comfortably, week by week, in the broadcasting channel's Top Twenty or even Top Ten programmes of the week.

Once this happy situation is achieved, then any adverse alteration to the format – a presenter or two dropped, the music changed, the transmission time altered – will result in public outcry, with letters to the press, television switchboards cluttered with indignant protests and vociferous complaints on those complaining TV shows. Gardeners can be very cross indeed when they are crossed.

There is the famous (and true) story of the high-powered television executive – an unfortunate soul who thought that gardening was really rather boring – who arbitrarily changed the transmission time of one of those much-loved, long-running series. He rode out the predictable storm of protest with disdain and indifference, but caved in completely when, in the bar of the Royal Opera House, Covent Garden, he was cornered by opera-goers, who also happened to be keen gardeners, demanding to know what on earth he thought he was doing with 'their' gardening programme. Within weeks, the show was restored to its familiar slot in the Friday night schedule.

I have referred to 'the formula', but in fact there is no set text, no list of characters, no budget and no single approach which will guarantee success, thank goodness.

The gardening audience, although potentially very large indeed, varies enormously. There are those people, for example, who are just taking their first tentative steps towards our national hobby, and simply want to know how they can set about transforming a pile of builder's rubble into something attractive, without being baffled by the finer points of horticulture. At the other end of the scale, there will be the self-taught experts, with thirty or more years' experience, who refer to all the plants in their garden by their Latin botanical names, open their garden twice a year to the public under the National Gardens scheme, but are puzzled, perhaps, by the woeful mis-behaviour of one particular specimen.

There is also the question of money, of course – many gardeners have to be extremely cost-conscious, there are others for whom cash presents no problem. I came across a man in Swansea who propagated all his own plants, didn't buy expensive chemicals or fertilizers and went in for recycling materials in a big way – he had dismantled an old unwanted bed and made a pergola from the timber frame and the corner supports for a cold frame from the iron legs. The horsehair stuffing of the mattress was used as a mulch for runner beans and the linings for several hanging baskets. He was still puzzling over what to do with the springs when I left him. On the other hand, there was a lady in Shropshire who spent her weekends touring specialist nurseries all over the country and reckoned, on a conservative estimate, that she had spent £30,000 on choice plants for her garden over the last seven years.

How do you, as a programme maker, put together something which will appeal to all these tastes and bank balances, without bewildering the beginner or boring the veteran? The matter becomes even more complicated when you want to launch a new series – you have to come up with a new formula, which will distinguish your programme from anything else put out, past or present, by your rivals on the other channels.

Garden Club, made by HTV (West) from Bristol and commissioned and transmitted by Channel Four Television, has, I think, overcome these problems and quickly become very much a gardeners' favourite. It first reached the small screen in early spring 1991 and now, in 1993, is beginning its third season. Its viewing figures have been quite remarkable – in its first year, several of the programmes within the infant series pulled in the largest audiences ever claimed by Channel Four's gardening programmes over the last decade.

It is interesting and instructive to try to analyse how this extra-ordinary show was put together and how its success was achieved. Channel Four does not actually make most of the programmes which it transmits – in the jargon of the television business it is a publisher and transmitter of programmes, fostering other people's work and

presenting it to the public. The channel's prime movers are its commissioning editors, who collect other people's ideas, or come up with their own, then farm out and finance those ideas with other companies – either major broadcasting companies like HTV, or with smaller, independent companies who tend to make one series, or even one programme, at a time. Gardening comes within the remit of Channel Four's Education Department and the commissioning editor for gardening (among many other things) is Sue Shephard.

Sue had looked at other gardening programmes – and decided that there was something missing. She had always been struck by the fact that all gardeners were both enthusiastic and generous – prepared to share ideas, cuttings, even plants with each other. In a sense, there already was an informal 'club' to which anyone who was interested in gardens or plants automatically belonged. The new programme was to feature this interchange of ideas, and the title suggested itself – *Garden Club*.

Roy Lancaster, Linda Gummery and Matthew Biggs.

Sue took her idea to Derek Clark, then Director of Programmes at HTV. Bristol already had a considerable track record with gardening programmes for Channel Four, notably with a long-running series on organic gardening variously entitled *All Muck and Magic*, *More Muck and Magic* and *Loads More Muck and Magic*. They agreed that they wanted a programme which would travel, week by week, to different parts of the country and would feature, to a very high degree, the 'ordinary' gardeners whose gardens were being visited. Yes, of course there would be expert presenters who would disentangle the amateur gardeners' problems, give advice, identify mysterious species – but those presenters would also encourage the gardeners themselves to offer advice and opinon from their own practical experience. It was to be, if you like, not just lessons, but an amiable collective educational exercise. Put another way, it was to be a chat, or a series of chats, over a series of garden walls.

Roy Lancaster was the first of the names on the list of presenters. He was already very well known to viewers, having been associated for many years with the BBC's *Gardeners' World* programme, as well as having his own series, made by Granada Television and shown on Channel Four – *The Great Plant Collections*, an expedition covering some of the nation's most famous gardens and introducing the work of the great plant collectors, had been the most recent of these. Roy is a world-renowned plantsman, lecturer, writer and broadcaster and positively fizzes with enthusiasm over what he calls 'the three Ps' – plants, places and people. He is already up there with the legends of television gardening, such as Percy Thrower and Geoffrey Smith. Matthew Biggs was a new discovery – a young Kew-trained horticulturalist, originally from Leicester and proud of it, who had never been on network television before, but took to it like a duck to water. The first reporter on *Garden Club* was Rebecca Pow, who was trained at Wye College, has an environmental science degree and was already HTV's Environmental Reporter – latterly, Rebecca has become a mother and split the work with Linda Gummery. They all have different personalities, of course, but they all share certain qualities – they are enthusiastic, extremely knowledgeable in their fields, hard working and above all, they are geninely interested in the amateur gardeners they come across in the course of their travels.

There was one other essential condition set out right at the beginning for the making of *Garden Club* – each programme had to be taped as close as possible to the transmission date, so that viewers could sympathize and identify vividly with seasonal conditions, whether they produced monsoons in spring, droughts in summer, or gales in autumn. It is at this point that commissioning editors and heads of programmes gracefully retire (they have many other things to do) and leave the detail to the people who actually have to make the programmes, the production crew.

What happened, and continues to happen, goes something like this: six months prior to recording, which is invariably scheduled to start in the following spring, the producer/director, Adrian Brenard and the senior researcher Jo Readman, get into a huddle in Bristol and decide on the year's locations. They have to spread themselves, geographically, over the whole of the United Kingdom, partly to ensure that no region feels left out and partly to make certain that they cover as many different climatic and ground conditions as possible. For this reason, as the series has progressed, they have already visited many areas and are now on the lookout for places they haven't been to before. They tend to start in the south in the early spring, and work their way north thereafter, for obvious reasons – there wouldn't be much point in going up to Aberdeen in March in order to admire the frost.

Once each town or area is targeted, Jo Readman contacts as many people and as many organizations in each area as she can – garden clubs, specialist societies and the like – and also puts an advertisement in the local paper. Armed with names and addresses, she then sets off on a tour, devoting about a week to each place, to find the gardens and gardeners who will be asked to appear in the show. This is a very difficult task, for she must try to come up with five or six subjects for each programme – obviously the subjects within each programme must vary, so that she doesn't end up with half a dozen people who all want to talk about, say, leeks or chrysanthemums. Bear in mind also that Jo's preliminary forays take place in late autumn, so she has to visualize what is going to be happening there in spring and through summer.

Before a camera turns, the whole year's work is mapped out in broad detail: I mention this because there are always viewers/ gardeners who ring up after seeing the show on Channel Four on Friday evening and want to join in the fun the following week. They sometimes get quite upset when they are told that the team cannot change all their plans to get to Preston next week to see the finest tomatoes in Europe, or some such. If you think you have something interesting or unusual to offer and would like to be considered for the programme, then keep a sharp eye on your local paper, or get in touch with HTV in November, which is when they are laying their plans for the following spring and after.

Once production begins to roll in earnest, everything happens with breathtaking speed. Each show is shot on Thursday, Friday and Saturday – that three-day shoot also includes the crew's travel time from and back to their base in Bristol. It is all edited early the following week and is on the air the following Friday, by which time they are in the middle of the next shoot.

Each contributing gardener will have three, four or five minutes actual air time – one or two participants have said to me, somewhat ruefully, that 'if you blink when the show is on, you miss it'. Each of those pieces will take two or more hours to shoot – that ratio may sound extravagant to anyone not familiar with television techniques, but this sort of television is a much more complicated business than most people realize. The walk through the garden must be meticul-

Rebecca Pow agog
to learn the secrets
of propagating a
weigela.

ously planned and may have to be broken up into short sequences so
that the camera can be moved to get more interesting shots. While the
first camera concentrates on the gardener, the second one may be
prowling the garden to get other useful shots and close-ups which will
be edited in later. Every plant discussed will have to be shot in
close-up and dwelt upon and discussed long enough for its name to be
superimposed on the screen in post-production. Microphones will
have to be put in the most unlikely places so that they will be unobtrusive and yet pick up clearly every word that is spoken.

Picture the poor gardener, then, who has no previous experience
of television – with an alien microphone stuffed up his shirt or a
strange boom hovering just above his head, a probing camera following his every move and half a dozen people he has only just met
watching silently and intently only a few feet away. He has to walk
around his garden, to a carefully preplanned choreography, stopping
and starting lots of times, trying to remember what has been said and
what has not been said each time. He may have to repeat the same
answer to the same question several times if, for example, an
unexpected car goes by, a telephone rings, or a pneumatic drill erupts
in the street outside. He has to show plants to the presenter in such a
way that the camera can see them as well, which can sometimes result

Getting it taped . . .
the crew are the
unsung heroes of
Garden Club.

in quite extraordinary contortions. In the middle of all this whirl of confusion, he is constantly told to 'be natural – try to pretend we aren't here'. It is an enormous tribute to the general resilience of gardeners, and to the skills and sympathy of the three presenters and the HTV crew that everything always seems to work out so well.

As I've said, Adrian Brenard and his team have a very tight schedule and simply cannot afford to waste a minute. If it is lashing with rain on the morning they are due to shoot a long sequence in an idyllically beautiful garden, the chances are that they will just have to go ahead and shoot. Oddly enough, electronic cameras don't seem to pick up the rain and several times I've stood on location and watched everyone suffer – then seen the results on the screen and wondered momentarily if it was the same place.

There is, then, very little room for manoeuvre, which means that sometimes they have to shoot the spring bedding which hasn't quite sprung, or the rhododendrons which are ever so slightly past their

peak – I've heard, several times, a gardener lamenting to the crew – 'if only you could have been here last week . . . or next week'. In fact, I think all this is part of the programme's charm – and perhaps one of the reasons for its success. This is *real* gardening, with all its ups and downs, its triumphs and its mini-tragedies, its smiles and its tears – we've not being asked to admire, relentlessly, the sort of immaculate, expensive, disheartening garden of Eden which is pictured on the front of chocolate boxes and in those glossy magazines and colour supplements. The gardens you see on *Garden Club* represent, by and large, the sort of garden *you* could have, with a bit of know-how and a lot of effort.

     Many people think that it takes a lifetime to acquire the skills to make and maintain a beautiful garden, but I have been astounded, time and time again, by meeting folk who have done it, by themselves, in a short space of time. There was a young couple in Oxford, for example, who, starting as absolute beginners, had transformed a con-

Roy Lancaster rehearses his 'Plant of the Week' before the camera starts to roll.

Roy, Rebecca and
Matthew and that
special sundial
from the familiar
opening sequence
of *Garden Club*.

crete jungle into a wonderful garden, cleverly designed on a narrow,
sloping site and bursting with almost two thousand different plants.
Nowadays they open their garden twice a year to the public under the
National Gardens Scheme and sell over a thousand small plants they
have propagated themselves to raise money for charity. They've done
all that in just six years. They are exceptional people, of course, but
there have been many others who have built up gardens anyone
would be proud of in two, three or four years – you will see them, time
and time again, on the programme. It is all quite inspirational and
means that there is hope for us all.

If you enjoy *Garden Club* and you regard television gardening as
something more than a spectacular sport, then you should know
about Gardening Club, which is run by Channel Four. You pay £12.50
to join and that entitles you to get all the back-up material – factsheets,
leaflets, newsletters – for all the year's gardening programmes on the
channel, not just *Garden Club*. It's not just a question of checking up on
the plant name that flashed by too quickly on the screen for you to
write it down, or having an autographed photograph of your favourite
presenter – there are good, detailed notes on the themes tackled, lists
of plants to be seen on the programme – and others that may not have
found their way on to the screen – booklists, addresses of nurseries
which can supply the plants you have seen and offers on garden tools
and equipment. You make your cheque out to Channel Four and send
it to:

Gardening Club
PO Box 4000
Cardiff CF5 2XT

Or you can use your Access or Visa card and call 0222 578666, during
office hours.

There are also occasional meetings where you might get a chance to
meet the presenters and the production team, ask questions, put
forward your own point of view about topics covered, or not covered,
by the series. I remember being at one of these meetings, in Norwich,
when a member of the audience, obviously bursting with indignation,
finally got up to ask her question – why was it, she demanded, that the
programme only lasted for a paltry half-hour? Why didn't they let it
run for an hour?

Preliminaries: Soil and Climate

Look to the soil

For several years, across the 1980s, there was a long-running and oft-repeated gardening series on Channel Four called *Gardeners' Calendar*. The programmes were filmed entirely at the Royal Horticultural Society's garden at Wisley, near Guildford, in Surrey. The series was introduced by actress and RHS member Hannah Gordon and the presenters were the heads of departments, the supervisors and the foremen of the RHS staff. It was a highly popular series and there were very few complaints from viewers as they watched the professionals get on with their work. There was however one quiet but persistent niggle – 'It must be so easy to garden with soil like that, muttered one or two disgruntled souls. 'They should come here and try and work on *my* soil.' I produced the series, so I had to deal with the niggles, when they arrived in letter form, as best I could.

Now Wisley is, of course, not just a national, but a world showcase of horticultural expertise and the soil there has been worked over with tender loving care by generations of gardeners, grafting away since the turn of the century, so it is hardly surprising that a spade goes into the ground like a knife through butter, and what comes up is a spadeful of lovely looking rich, crumbly, dark earth – the stuff that gardeners' dreams are made of. Things are not what they seem though, for Wisley's soil is, for the most part, a thin, acid sand that carries with it a host of horticultural problems which are not immediately apparent to the naked eye, or to the questing television camera.

You could not accuse *Garden Club* of glamourizing the good earth – they travel the country from week to week, so we see an enormous variety of soils, many of which started out as gardeners' nightmares. In Coventry, one allotment we saw had originally been that heavy clay which seems to weigh a ton for each spadeful in spring and can set to a concrete-like hardness in a dry summer. In Cornwall, a gardener new to the hobby was faced with the prospect of a thin acid sand, contaminated with copper from an abandoned mine. A young couple in Swansea had built their house on a plinth of free hardcore, which turned out to be slag from an iron furnace – where the plinth turned into a rockery, they were finding it difficult to grow the plants they wanted. The same unfortunate folk had an embankment on one side of their garden which consisted entirely of coal dust, the legacy of a neighbouring railway marshalling yard, long gone, but not forgotten.

A lady in Southampton had a garden whose soil was barely visible between large round stones – it was known by the locals as Brighton Beach. A fanatical gardener in Shrewsbury found he had a clause in the deeds of his house, forbidding him to extract sand and gravel – not surprising really, since that was all there was to begin with – sand and gravel.

Only the fortunate few inherit perfect soil. It usually has to be worked with and worked on. What the experience of all those *Garden Club* gardeners tells us, triumphantly, is that it can be done, no matter how formidable the problems may seem to begin with.

Clay soils

The most notorious and intractable soil is that known as heavy clay. All soil is a mixture of rock particles, decaying organic matter, air and water. In clay, the rock particles are close together and they hold the water very tightly, so that it can be heavy and sticky to dig at the best of times and well-nigh impossible to penetrate when it is very dry in summer. In winter, on the other hand, you may find that a heavy clay soil will be waterlogged.

When Jean Rawlinson moved into her house in Maghull, near Southport, thirty-five years ago, she found she had all she wanted – a large back garden, full of potential, sweeping quite steeply up to the towpath of the Leeds and Liverpool Canal. The trouble was, it was also full of that old favourite of so many new householders – compacted clay and builder's rubble. Gradually, she and her husband Alan cleared the rubble by hand and barrow. In their case, because the site was naturally self-draining, there was no need to dig drainage ditches or lay drainage pipes – that is something that you might have to bear in mind if you find yourself up against the clay problem.

It is a good idea to dig over clay, when it is diggable, in the autumn and let the winter frosts and rains break down the clods and lumps for you. This is exactly what Jean did – at one stage, incidentally, letting her enthusiasm run away with her and sticking the fork through her foot. She ended up a patient in the hospital where she worked as a nurse. Do take care – garden forks can be dangerous.

Clay needs to be opened up and this is best done by adding organic matter – some form of manure or compost – and coarse grit or sharp sand, to help drainage. Don't, whatever you do, use soft

Jean Rawlinson's
splendid garden at
Maghull, near
Southport, in late
spring.

builder's sand, as one unwary *Garden Club* gardener did. He found that it merely improved the concrete impression which clay can give in the summer.

The Rawlinsons planted potatoes everywhere at first, to clean up the soil and help to improve its texture – an old trick. 'We gave them to all our neighbours and ate potatoes until we had them coming out of our ears,' said Jean, 'and then we still had to take them to the tip by the van load.'

Once all this work is done, then clay soils, opened up and combined with suitable fertilizers, can actually be very good, since they are often rich in minerals, and nutrients are not leached away too quickly by heavy rainfall. They do tend to be cold soils though, and may take some time to warm up in early spring. You may find, therefore, that early sowings won't work too well, unless you warm up the soil first, with cloches or some form of clear polythene covering. Those gardeners on the allotment in Coventry did that – and also grew plants such as cabbages, in pots under cover first, rather than sowing in the open ground.

I've used the saga of Jean and Alan Rawlinson because they started all those years ago knowing very little about gardening, but tackled the clay in textbook fashion and now have a garden which is one of the most beautiful I have ever seen. You can see it too, if you are up in that direction in May, when they open the garden to the public for two Sundays, in the National Gardens Scheme. They had 1660 people through this year and I'm sure a lot of them must have said to themselves, 'If only I had soil like that – they should come and try and work in my garden.'

Sandy soils

At the opposite end of the scale from the heavy clays, you have very sandy soils, which can present their own catalogue of problems. In sandy soil, the rock particles are comparatively large and water drains away quickly, so they are easy to dig and they do warm up early in spring, which means that you can sow early. There was a classic example of the comparison between clay and sand in that *Garden Club* programme from Coventry, which was shot and shown in early spring: there were two plots, on different allotments, but not too far apart – the one on clay and another one on sand. Both had been worked on and both now had good soil, but the allotmenteer on sand was still able to get his vegetables on the move a couple of weeks before his opposite number on the clay.

The major disadvantage of sandy soil is that water tends to pour though those rock particles very quickly, taking with it the food and minerals that plants need. At the RHS garden at Wisley, they have to spend an inordinate amount of money and time to ensure that the soil is fed and watered. Bulky organic material, fertilizer and grit are added, and irrigation is copious and constant, especially during long dry periods, when there is a danger that sandy soils will become more and more a desert. If you have the problem, then you will have to do the same thing. The initial solution to the quite different problems of unyielding clay and loose sandy soils is thus, strangely enough, the same – add organic matter.

Organic matter matters

Only a few years ago, if you had said 'organic matter' to a gardener, you would probably have meant peat, but nowadays, you have to be more careful. Peat can be used, and still is, but worries about the depletion of the wetland habitats from which peat is extracted mean that many conservation-minded gardeners now look for some alternative. Well-rotted garden compost, or leaf mould, both of which you can make yourself, will do nicely. Animal manure, bulked up with straw and well rotted, is good too – horses produce the richest manure, followed by pigs, cows and poultry. I remember, years ago, gardeners in my street at home watching the horse-drawn milk cart, with eyes like hawks, brush and shovel close at hand. Over the last couple of years, I have seen the same gleam in the eye of *Garden Club* followers when they talk about the local stables. Once gardener told me wistfully of an article he had read in his paper about a zoo in the Netherlands, which had started marketing elephant dung in five-litre presentation buckets – very good for roses and bedding plants, they claimed. Tiger droppings were another possibility, apparently – not only good for the soil, the zoo keepers claimed, but kept rabbits and cats away. Other possibilities include spent mushroom compost, seaweed, spent hops, pulverized bark, dried sewage sludge and shoddy, which is wool waste. Some of these products and by-products are more easily available in certain areas than in others, as *Garden Club* has shown. Down in Penzance, they had easy access to seaweed. In Kent, spent hops were not too difficult to get hold of, while shoddy is the stuff they go for near the woollen mills of West Yorkshire.

The organic gardener has another alternative, a process known as 'green manuring'. We saw a team of keen green gardeners in the West Country, who have organized themselves in the Bath Organic Group (curiously acronymed BOG), to promote organic gardening. They maintain the fertility of the soil on their communal allotments by using heavy dressings of home-made compost and green manure. They sow green crops such as cereal rye (*Secale ceriale*). Winter field beans, an agricultural variety of the broad bean (*Vicia faba*) and Winter tares (*Vicia sativa*) on the bare ground in autumn, and dig them in during spring, before they flower, thus providing decaying organic matter and food for following crops of vegetables. There are other greens, which can be sown and dug in at different times of the year – it is important that you choose an appropriate type for the season.

There is a useful and cheap pamphlet which explains the whole process in great detail – *Gardening with Green Manures*, written by members of the Henry Doubleday Research Association and available for 50p, plus 30p postage, from Chase Organics (GB) Ltd, Coombelands House, Coombelands Lane, Addlestone, Weybridge KT15 1HY.

When you can describe your soil as a friable loam, then you have arrived at the gardener's nirvana – loam is the perfect recipe, a blend of sand and clay particles, wrapped up in organic matter. It will dig easily, retain its moisture well and, with the appropriate fertilizer, will be good for most crops. The next thing you have to worry about is whether you have acid or alkaline soil.

The acid test

When Roy Lancaster gives one of his now famous lectures on plant hunting in China, he often slips in one of his slides of *Rhododendron cephalanthum*, showing pinkish-white flowers and growing quite happily out of a limestone cliff in the Cangshan mountains of Western Yunan. The picture brings forth gasps of amazement from the spellbound crowd, because gardeners have been told, time and time again, that rhododendrons are *not* happy in limey or alkaline

If you do not have the right sort of soil, you can still grow acid-loving plants, like this azalea, in containers.

soils and will only flourish on acid soil. In most cases, this is true, and Roy's plant is one of those delightfully mischievous exceptions to the rule.

If you live in limestone country and you want to grow rhododendrons, then in most cases you have to provide them with their own private enclosed patches of acid soil – perhaps containers of some sort, if the plants are small enough, or raised self-contained beds, or pits of acid soil sunk in the ground and protected underground by perforated polythene. There are other plants, such as camellias, azaleas, magnolias, some heathers, blueberries and blue hydrangeas which are acid-loving and lime-hating.

At the other end of the scale, there are plants which behave in exactly the opposite way – they are lime-loving and acid-hating and include in their number, as you might expect, many flowers from the limestone mountains of the world.

By far the simplest way to see whether your local soil is acid or alkaline is to walk around your neighbourhood and look over garden walls and fences – if lots of people seem to be growing rhododendrons without too much trouble, and all the hydrangeas are blue, the problem is solved.

You can also buy equipment to test your own soil – there are various reasonably inexpensive versions of an electronic meter with a thin probe which you push into the ground and read off the result on a dial, and there are kits where you usually collect tiny samples of soil, mix them up in a test tube with the chemical provided and match the colour which emerges with a chart from the kit. You can also send samples of your soil for professional analysis. However you do it, you will eventually come up with what is called a pH reading.

The principle is simple enough – pH is an indicator of the degree of acidity or alkalinity of the soil. The table of possibilities looks something like this:

4.5	extremely acid
4.5–5.0	very strong acid
5.1–5.5	strongly acid
5.6–6.0	medium acid
6.1–6.5	slightly acid
6.6–7.3	neutral
7.4–8.0	mildly alkaline
8.1–9.0	strongly alkaline
9.1 and above	extremely alkaline

Most of the books tell us that it would be extremely unusual for a reading from a garden to come out below 4.5 or above 8.5 and most plants – and that includes vegetables and fruit – grow best on slightly acid soil, from Ph 6 to 6.5. Some gardeners worry a great deal about all this and strive to get their pH into the required parameters – many don't bother too much, knowing from practical experience that plants are remarkably tolerant.

One or two people warned me that pH measurement is fraught with problems which don't always get into the gardening books – you should, for example, test different parts of your garden to get a complete picture. A gardener in Oxford told the tale of the dying Japanese azalea – although planted in the approved acidic soil, it had suffered from the lime leaching out of the cement on a nearby brick wall. The soil had, of course, turned alkaline. Adding peat to soil will temporarily increase acidity – one gardener whose soil was in the region of 6.3 to 7.0 on the pH scale, found that the reading fell to 5 temporarily when he dug in peat, although the effect gradually wore off. The electrical probe meters work more accurately in the close-textured soils. If you don't wash the probe and then buff it up with the scouring pad the manufacturers usually provide, you can get wildly inaccurate readings.

If you are unhappy with the pH of your soil, you can change it. On the sandy soil of that Coventry allotment, they added lime in the autumn, allowing the rain to wash it in – this brought the pH up to exactly what they wanted, a reading of 6.8. You can use ground chalk (calcium carbonate) or garden lime (calcium hydroxide). If you want to reduce the pH, in other words to acidify your soil, you can add sulphur or aluminium sulphate.

There is really very little point though, in trying to effect huge changes – it would be a very expensive business and lead only to temporary alteration. If you have what some people might consider excessively alkaline soil, then you can chose to live with it and enjoy the plants that will flourish there. In the first series of *Garden Club*, in the spring of 1991, the programme visited a garden at Rhos on Sea, in North Wales, where the pH level was 7.9. The couple there had a wonderful terraced garden, with shrub and flower borders in colour themes – yellow, blue and white, grey and pink. They had picked their plants carefully, going through the reference books for lime-tolerant species and varieties, and put the whole together with consummate good taste and skill.

Coping with the climate

We now come to the problems for gardeners posed by the British climate. The majority of our garden plants start to grow when the soil temperature (about a foot down) reaches a steady 6°C in early spring – and stop growing when it drops below 6°C in the autumn. This is the period known as the growing season and it averages out over Britain at about 250 days per year. Broadly speaking, the further north you garden, the shorter the growing season. In some sheltered parts of Cornwall, that season can sometimes be extended to an almost incredible 360 days – imagine, a gardening year with less than a week when things aren't growing – when do they get time to browse by the fire with next year's seed catalogues? Up in the Highlands of Scotland, however, that season can be as short as 150 days.

The pioneering programmes in the very first series of *Garden Club*, in the early spring of 1991, illustrated those south/north growing seasons in graphic detail. First, there was the Midlands, which looked sodden and unkind in early March, although that didn't stop the gardeners there showing how they sowed and planted their early vegetables. The following week, the programme came from Penzance, in Cornwall, where, unusually, they had just had snow, but the sea was blue, the sun shone, and the season was four weeks ahead of the Midlands. In week three, the production team were in Newcastle upon Tyne – here the season was six weeks behind Cornwall. All this showed quite clearly that your gardening year must be adjusted to how far north, or south, you live, and not by any flatly stated dates for action in a book.

The growing season is further curtailed by frosts, of course – again, the further north you are, the later the last spring frosts and the earlier the first frosts of autumn. You don't put out your summer bedding plants permanently until the danger of frost has gone and that date can vary considerably wherever you happen to be. The simplest and I think the best solution to this problem I ever heard came from a man in Southport, who said that he always waited until the swallows arrived – what he called his 'golden day' was usually the 15th of May. Don't bother too much then, about the pundits and the weather forecasters – just leave it to the birds.

Rainfall

Then there is the West/East divide to consider. Generally speaking, the western parts of Britain take the brunt of the prevailing winds surging in endlessly from the Atlantic – these winds bring a lot of rain and the western half of Britain is wetter than the eastern parts. Until comparatively recently, this didn't seem to matter very much, since the whole of Britain was, by European standards, very wet. But for some Eastern parts of Britain, water has become a scarce and valuable commodity.

No one knows whether these new conditions are the first manifestations of the much heralded global warming, or whether we are simply experiencing a period of prolonged drought, but either way, *Garden Club* has come up with some startling examples of the difficulties posed for gardeners by lack of essential water for irrigation – and some of the solutions that gardeners have come up with.

In Norfolk, we saw a gardener who had given up on his local supply for his garden and had constructed a rainwater collection system of his own. He had tapped into the guttering around his and his neighbour's house and channelled what rain there was into four forty-gallon drums, with an overflow system from one drum to another. The drums were raised from the ground on concrete blocks and had taps at the bottom, so that the watering-can could be filled without difficulty. A similar system was based on the guttering around his greenhouse at the bottom of the garden – two more forty-gallon drums collected water here. All the drums were full and he and his neighbour had the satisfaction of a private reservoir of two hundred and forty gallons of water for their gardens in the middle of a drought and a seemingly endless hose-pipe ban. You can buy plastic water butts from the garden centre, but this Norfolk gardener had baulked at the expense of that and had bought old soy sauce drums at an auction, drilled out holes and put in spigots at the bottom of each one himself. During the summer, he put baskets of trailing lobelia on top of the drums, to conceal the rather ugly barrels.

Up in the dry north–east, another determined gardener had taught himself the mysterious art of water-divining and discovered an underground supply in his own garden by digging a six-foot well. He used two electric welding rods instead of the traditional diviners' witch-hazel wand to look for water and practised on Sunday mornings

A coastal garden in Ilfracombe which requires salt and wind-tolerant plants.

before the family got up – he wasn't sure that it was going to work and he didn't want to look a fool in front of the wife and kids. I am duty bound to reveal no further details, since he fears that the local water company might have something to say on the matter. Needless to say, this particular episode did not feature on television.

There are other, slightly more orthodox, methods of coping with the problem of water shortage. A Suffolk gardener had cut plastic litre bottles in half, and sunk the top half of each bottle, neck-down, into the ground by the side of favourite plants – when a plant showed signs of distress, he poured water down the makeshift funnel, so that it went straight to the roots. Obviously, you use only a fraction of the water that you might otherwise have done, scattering it with gay abandon from a watering-can. A similar solution is to drill tiny holes in the bottom and sides of a plastic bottle and bury the whole thing, the right way up this time, with just the neck protruding above the surface of the soil. In either case, you must have some idea of the rooting habits of the plants you are trying to help, so that the water is actually getting to the right level.

There were several examples, within the first two years of *Garden Club*, of gardeners in the dry areas of Britain who had simply adapted to circumstances and begun to experiment successfully with plants which will grow in this sort of climate – tender plants, often from the Mediterranean regions, sometimes from further afield. We are seeing many more examples of cistus, ceanothus, olearia, lavatera and abutilons than we used to.

There are other general climatic factors which will effect the way you garden. Coastal areas tend to be warmer in winter and cooler in summer than areas inland, because of the moderating effect of the sea on temperature although salt-laden winds can play havoc with some sorts of plant. Along certain parts of the west coast, the Gulf Stream creates conditions where, with appropriate shelter belts of trees or shrubs, tender and even sub-tropical plants can grow. One thinks of famous showplace gardens such as Tresco, in the Scilly Islands, Port Logan and Inverewe, on the west coast of Scotland, but I for one was startled to see, in a *Garden Club* programme, that Llandundo, in North Wales, benefits to a certain extent from this warmer flow of water.

Cities tend to be warmer than the surrounding countryside and you will often find the most surprisingly exotic plants growing in sheltered spots in, say, Birmingham, Nottingham or London. In practical terms, city gardeners can often start their gardening, the soil warmed up, a week or two before people only a few miles out.

Tranquil countryside near Wenlock Edge, Shropshire. They can get fierce winds out of the east hereabouts.

The ups and downs of altitude

Besides latitude and longitude, altitude can make a startling difference to your growing season. The average temperature drops
by some 2°F for each 800 feet of altitude, and that can make several
days' difference to the beginning and end of the growing season.
Garden Club has come up with several variations on this theme, but I
think my favourite and most succinct summing up of the situation
came from a gardener at the bottom of the Welsh valleys, near Swansea, who said that when he went to see a friend and fellow gardener at
the top of the valley, 900 feet higher up, 'it was two overcoats colder'.
In Shropshire, there was a difference of two weeks in the growing
season between two places only a few miles apart – the difference was
that one garden was down in the valley, by the River Wye, and the
other one was 900 feet up, overlooking Wenlock Edge.

Sheltering from the wind

Although, as I have already mentioned, the prevailing winds tend
to be those from south-west, punishing winds and damaging
gales can comes at you from almost any angle. One or two of those
gardeners in Shropshire had startling stories to tell of rhododendrons
being blown out of the ground and greenhouses being carried away by
ferocious winds from the east. 'There's nothing much in the way of
mountains between us and Russia', one of them told me – and if you
look at a map that is true. Every gardener in the South and South-East
remembers the Great Gale of October 1987, which brewed up swiftly
and spectacularly to the south of the British Isles in the Bay of Biscay
and cut a swathe of destruction through the South-East of England,
skittling over nineteen million trees.

    All that was dramatic stuff, of course, but every garden vulner-
able to winds needs some sort of protection. A solid wall is not
necessarily the answer, since the wind can spill over it like a giant
invisible wave and cause huge turbulence on the other side. A shelter
belt of trees or hedging will filter the worst effects of the wind. One
desperate gardener near the Norfolk coast found that he simply could
not establish such a shelterbelt – the trees and hedges that he tried to

plant were scorched and killed and sometimes blown away. The answer here, as elsewhere in similar situations, was to erect a screen of plastic mesh or webbing on stout posts, which will provide the filtering and sheltering effect so that the hedge or young tree shelter belt can establish itself to leeward.

Ray Robbins' hedge is a delight to the eye *and* serves a useful purpose. Ilfracombe, Devon.

Particular cases

I have been writing in general terms about general problems raised by the British climate, but every region of Britain – and every individual garden – has its own series of climatic pluses and bonuses. Some people go to extraordinary lengths to buy the house with perfect gardening potential. I met one man, just outside Norwich, who had found the perfect spot – a steeply sloping, south-facing garden, entirely surrounded, at a distance, by other gardens' sheltering trees. South-facing gardens are obviously warm, and a sloping garden facing the sun is actually warmer than a flat garden of similar aspect. The problem was that the house in the middle of this idyllic spot was on shaky foundations and proved to be all but unmortgageable. Of course, the gardener moved in.

Not all of us would take that sort of risk with the house, but if you care about these things, it is worth looking carefully at the garden, as well as the mortgage, before you buy. I have met several gardeners who, in looking at a new house and garden they were interested in, would take a compass along, in case it was a dull day, so that they could calculate just what the sun would do to the garden during the course of the day. Which were the south-facing walls? Where were the areas of permanent shade, of partial shade, of full sun? You can also learn a lot by looking at existing plants, shrubs and trees – what is flourishing and what looks in poor health? Is the garden exposed to wind? Are there boggy, badly drained areas?

The vast majority of people will buy the house first, and then make the best they can of the garden that goes with it. The first horticultural step, I would suggest, is to look around the neighbourhood and find some experienced gardeners who will be able to tell you about local soil and weather conditions. These things can be very complex – one regional example from the *Garden Club* file will suffice.

In and around Grimsby, on the east coast, local gardeners can tell you of totally different soil conditions and types only a few miles one from another – there are chalk soils, acid soils, sandy soils and clay – the whole encyclopaedia. The River Humber has a pronounced effect on climatic conditions – this large body of water acts rather like a thermostat, keeping the temperature a touch milder in winter and a little bit cooler in summer than it otherwise would be. North of the river, it is appreciably wetter than to the south. The further inland you go, towards the Wolds, the colder it can get. There is often snow on the hills in winter, visible from gardens by the sea or river, which rarely get even a frost.

Grimsby is a particularly interesting case, but every region of the country has its own complicated pattern of soil and climate, which the keen gardener – with a little help from his or her friends – will gradually unravel. There is a further, fascinating challenge, and that is the mini-geography and microclimates of your own garden, which will be subtly different from everyone else's. Those problems you must sort out for yourself, usually by trial and error.

Spring

Signs

When does spring begin? If you go by the book, then the vernal equinox, usually round about the 21 March, is the beginning of spring. Ask a gardener when his or her spring begins and you will get a much more interesting answer to the question.

There is a rhododendron, called *R.* 'Praecox', originally bred in Lancashire in the middle of the last century by crossing *R. ciliatum* with *R. dauricum*. Being a loyal Lancastrian, I have one in my garden and it usually puts out a courageous and colourful display of lilac flowers in early March. When that happens, I always feel that spring has begun in my part of the world. I was delighted to hear, from several *Garden Club* members that they too had personal choices for that magic moment when winter turns to spring and there is hope after all. Several people in the south mentioned camellias; one gardener in Surrey always looks out for the flowering of a Japanese wild apricot, called *Prunus mume* 'Omoi-no-mama'; bulbs, of course are popular, with early crocuses, narcissi, scillas and chionodoxas often mentioned. A gardener in Oxford told me that his choice would always be a combination of white snowdrops and yellow winter aconites – he was a hospital porter at one time and when he saw those flowers in bloom by a sheltered wall of the Nuffield Hospital he knew the worst of the winter was over.

For those who regard gardening as a duty rather than a pleasure, I suppose spring is that time when the soil temperature has reached the magical 6°C, the grass starts to grow and you discover that you have forgotten to have the lawnmower serviced over the winter.

Spring greens: the lawn

Jack Tomlins is known as 'the man who mows his lawn twice a day' – that was the headline over a story about him in the gardening press once. His tiny front garden in Shrewsbury is wonderful and already quite famous. He regularly wins prizes for it, and has had photographs of it published in several of the national gardening magazines. He is the current Gardener of the Year, a prestigious award given annually by the Garden News. There is a picture on Jack's sideboard of

Jack Tomlins' front lawn – raised to the height of perfection from unpromising beginnings.

the late, much-revered Percy Thrower, admiring the bedding plants, the immaculate topiary, and the absolutely splendid lawn.

Like many people, Jack inherited what he described as a scruffy, weedy overgrown lawn when he first moved into his bungalow. He didn't dig it up and start again by sowing grass seed or laying turf, but nursed the old lawn back to life by simply mowing and weeding. Nowadays, in spring, he scarifies the grass, giving it a good raking over with a spring tine rake, then goes over the whole area with a garden fork sticking in the fork to make holes for drainage and aeration. He feeds, with a high nitrogen feed and uses a selective weed killer a week or so later. The feeding and weedkilling go on regularly through the season.

Jack reckons that the real key to a good lawn is mowing technique – he starts in early spring with the blades of the mower set high, then gradually lowers them as the season progresses, until he has exactly the short cut he wants – about half an inch or so. He uses an eight-blade cylinder mower which he says gives a finer, more even cut and swears that a cylinder mower is the only machine which will give you proper stripes. That story about mowing the lawn twice a day is a joke really – what Jack does is to mow his lawn up and down, and then go over it lightly with a rake, so that the stronger grasses stand up again. Then he mows it from side to side, so that he gets the chequerboard effect that you may well have seen at Wembley, when the television commentators always admire the pitch just before the Cup Final. Jack trims the edges of the lawn with edging shears, just to finish the job off. His soil is sand and gravel, so he has to water frequently.

The British make something of a religion out of grass – I don't think you'll find any other country where it is worshipped so much. Being a religion, there are often theological disputes among members over certain points of doctrine. One of the most frequent disagreements concerns the problem of what to do with grass cuttings. Some people collect the clippings and put them on their compost heaps. Others swear that this is a waste of time, effort and resources, and say that you don't need to box off and collect clippings, but should leave them where they fall, so that they can rot back into the lawn – in effect, a form of green manuring. Both points of view crop up with bewildering regularity in magazines and on radio and television programmes, and among *Garden Club* gardeners and the problem is never resolved, so I think the answer is to follow your own inclination, with one warning – even if you are of the leave-the-clippings-where-they-are school of thought, you must rake them up and get rid of them if the grass was long and wet when it was cut and the clippings emerge from the mower in great lumps.

If you have a largish lawn and you follow the recommendations on the packets of proprietary lawn lotions and potions, for the lawn's annual treatment, you are likely to spend a great deal of money. I came across several gardeners, in different parts of the country, who simply scatter a general fertilizer, such as Growmore, very thinly over the lawn in spring, and get rid of the worst weeds, such as dandelions and plantains, by hand, with an old knife or dibber. One man actually said to me that he *didn't* want a picture-book lawn and he quite liked the daisies and other minor weeds: he mowed his lawn every five days or so, watered it from time to time and that was that. It looked pretty good to me and did what lawns are supposed to do – provided

something pleasant to walk on and set off the rest of the garden to perfection.

There certainly seems to have been a move away from straight edges to lawns and almost everyone I spoke to had scalloped the edges of their lawn, using a hosepipe laid on the ground to mark out the curves edges – the sinuously arranged hose-pipe was then held in place by canes, and the new margins of the lawn cut out with one of those half-moon edging tools.

Spring is a good time of the year to sow or turf a new lawn. Newly sown grass or newly laid turf will wither and die if it is allowed to dry out and the theory is that our springs are generally damp enough to do the watering naturally. Autumn is the other approved period, for the same reasons. It was a *Garden Club* member in the North of England who pointed out that you could quite easily sow a lawn in the summer too – after all, the professionals who look after all the nations' football pitches have to do their sowing in the close season, in June, so that they are ready for the beginning of the season in mid-August. If it is a dry summer though, you will have a lot of watering to do.

A typical example of the scalloped lawn edges favoured by most of the Channel Four gardeners. The tree is *Cornus Controversa* 'Variegata'.

Spring bulbs

Galanthus nivalis is the botanical name for the common snowdrop and translates beautifully into 'the milk-white flower of the snow'. This is the plant which green-spears its way out of the soil, and often through the snow, in January, then drops its head to flower sometimes in February.

The first *Garden Club* programme of 1991 visited Colin Mason, who has an extraordinary collection of snowdrops, in Kenilworth. As is so often the case, what one might have thought of as a simple flower turns out to be a member of a large, complicated family – Colin Mason has almost two hundred different kinds of snowdrop in the collection, each one subtly different from the next – if you pick your plants carefully, from a specialist nursery, you could have snowdrops of one kind or another in bloom in your garden from late autumn of one year to late spring of the next.

The true snowdrop lover – the galanthophile – will point out some of the minute differences between one kind of snowdrop and another, perhaps the size of the smudge of green in or on the white flower, perhaps a difference in the length or breadth of the foliage. Most of us would be content to recognize – and grow – a handful of the various plants from within the family group.

Colin Mason recommends *Galanthus nivalis* 'Sam Arnott', a large and sturdy variety, reputed to smell of honey, *G.n.* 'Magnet' and *G.n.* 'Brenda Troyle'. I'm fond of *Galanthus nivalis* 'Scharlockii', discovered by one Julius Scharlock in Germany in the middle of the nineteenth century, but familiarly known as 'Donkey Ears', because of the shape of its bifurcated leaves. Then there is *Galanthus nivalis* 'Lutescens', which is most unusual in that it has yellow marks on its petals instead of the usual green. When it was first discovered up in Northumberland in the last century, the snowdrop sellers on the local markets used to throw them away, since they were thought to look sickly. Now you could well find yourself paying £7 for a single bulb.

Many of the rarer species and varieties can be expensive. At the Royal Horticultural Society's garden at Wisley, where they have a large collection of snowdrops scattered throughout an area known as the Wild Wood, they eventually had to replace the plant labels with names on them for tags with numbers. You had to ask for a map with a key to the numbers at the office, so that staff would know exactly who

was wandering about among their snowdrops because so many of the more exotic ones were being stolen.

Once snowdrops are settled in ground they like, they will thrive and multiply – so much so that they will have to be dug up and thinned out every three years or so, to prevent overcrowding. If you haven't got snowdrops and would like to get hold of some from your garden, late March or early April is the time to go begging from a neighbour or friend who has an abundant supply, for snowdrops are best transplanted 'in the green', that is to say, when the flowers are over but the green foliage is still there. If you buy packets of bulbs in the autumn, you may find that some of them have become too dry and your success rate may not be spectacular.

My friend the Oxford hospital porter was quite right – the combination of snowdrops and winter aconites is a splendid one. The up-turned buttercup-yellow flowers of the aconite, resting on a green ruff of leaves, are in complete contrast to the modest nodding white heads of snowdrops, but they do seem to go together quite beautifully if they are planted so that they produce pools of white and yellow. *Eranthis*

Winter aconites, snowdrops and hellebores help to cheer up dark days at the beginning of the year.

Narcissus
'February Gold' –
do not expect it to
flower until March.

hymalis is the common winter aconite, but nowadays you can buy not just them, but named garden hybrids, such as 'Glory' and 'Guinea Gold'.

The broad and generally accepted chronology of bulbs sweeps on, from snowdrops and aconites, through crocuses, snowflakes (*Leucojum vernum* – often confused with snowdrops by the beginner), iris, such as *Iris reticulata* and *Iris danfordiae*, scillas and chionodoxas, to the largest and unquestionably the most popular spring bulb of them all, the narcissi, or daffodils. If you include the narcissi such as 'Paper White', which we force for Christmas in the house, and take into account all those cut daffodils from warmer climes like Cornwall and the Scilly Islands that we buy in early spring, then think of the vast range of daffodils that you could have flowering in the garden from, say, February to the end of April, you can appreciate that narcissi are part of our lives for five or six months of the year.

They are a versatile breed, and can be used in almost every garden situation – in grass, under glass, in formal borders, as bedding plants, in rockeries and alpine gardens, in window-boxes and containers, by paths, among shrubs and in mixed or herbaceous borders – the list is almost endless.

The Royal Horticultural Society called the first conference on daffodils in 1884, in an attempt to sort out the vast confusion over type and nomenclature which already existed. Today, the family is officially classified into twelve groups, or divisions, ranging from trumpet daffodils of garden origin, through long cups and short cups, doubles, cyclamineus daffodils and the rest, to a catch-all category twelve which sweeps up anything not covered by the other eleven groups. The classification goes into great detail about the structure of the flower and it is useful to know, when you are browsing through catalogues, that the central part of the flower is called a trumpet if it is as long as, or longer than, the petals, and a cup if it is shorter and a corona if you want to use the correct botanical term. The petals aren't exactly petals to the botanist – they call them perianth segments, or corollas.

In spite of all this complex technical detail, daffodils are extremely easy to grow. Bulbs are generally on sale by September and once you have decided which ones you want and have bought them, they should be planted as soon as possible. They like well-drained soil, with plenty of rotted organic material incorporated in it. Unless they are in very poor soil, they don't require much in the way of fertilizer, although most people would scatter a little Growmore or bonemeal around at planting. Look at the bulb – if it is about five centimetres from tip to toe, then plant it fifteen centimetres down in reasonable soil, perhaps only ten centimetres down in a heavy clay soil.

After you have enjoyed the flowering of your daffodils, they will need further care . They should be dead-headed, so that the plant doesn't waste energy trying to seed. There is a minor problem now, especially for excessively tidy gardeners, for it is best to leave the foliage to die down naturally, so that the bulb builds up strength from the decay of this foliage for the next year. This dying down is not a pretty process and there was a time when people used to tidy up daffodils left *in situ* by trussing up this foliage with rubber bands, or would cut it off at the base. They would similarly be keen to mow over daffodils planted in grass. All they were doing with this excess zeal was slowly but surely killing off the plant. The RHS ran an experiment at their garden at Wisley, which finally convinced many people of the error of their ways – lines of daffodils were planted out down a grassy slope in the trials fields, one line was left to die down naturally, the next line was mowed two weeks after flowering, the next four weeks, the next six weeks. Over the ten years of the trial, the plants mowed early gradually weakened and died out – those mowed after two weeks quickest of all. The line that was left alone was still going strong at the end of the experiment.

Many gardeners I met like to buy different daffodils each year. In the first year they plant them in containers – large pots or tubs – and use them to brighten up the front of the house. Then, when they've seen and enjoyed the results in spring, they dead-head, move the containers to a discreet, shady corner of the garden and replant in the ground in the autumn, in groups according to type or variety and let them get on with it thereafter. Gardeners with smaller areas to play around in dig up their daffodils, heel them in to a small trench in a quiet spot and replant in September.

In spring 1991, *Garden Club* went to Northern Ireland and visited a world-famous professional daffodil breeder, Kate Reade. She showed Rebecca Pow just a few of the varieties she has produced, including 'Gypsy Queen', a pale yellow miniature, 'Foundling', a cyclamineus type with swept back white petals and a startling pink cup, and 'Gin and Lime', a bicolour trumpet which Kate described as cool and refreshing, 'just like the drink'. New daffodils are always being produced by breeders like Kate and a real aficionado will always want to go to the RHS Spring Shows in March and early April in London, or read up in the gardening magazines, about the newly introduced varieties. The newer the introduction, the more expensive the bulbs tend to be, so a lot of people wait a year or two, until the breeders have bulked up their supplies and passed them on into the more general trade.

The old favourites, of course, live on, in riotous good health, and I must confess a fondness for those big brassy golden trumpets such as 'Carlton', 'Golden Harvest', both introduced in the late 1920s and even 'King Alfred', whose bulbs, when they were first introduced in 1899, cost an incredible £10 each. 'Unsurpassable' is possibly the biggest of this particular bunch. At the other end of the scale, many *Garden Club* enthusiasts I spoke to love the tiny daffodils with the swept back corollas bred from the species *Narcissus cyclamineus* – 'Peeping Tom', 'Tête-à-tête. 'Dove Wings' and 'Jack Snipe'. Then there is 'February Gold', bred in Holland in 1923, by crossing *N. cyclamineus* with the wild daffodil, *Narcissus pseudonarcissus* – it might flower in Holland in February I suppose, but no one I've met in Britain expects to see it until March. *Narcissus bulbocodium*, the tiny hoop-petticoat daffodil, is much

Narcissus
cyclamineus 'Jack
Snipe'.

treasured in many gardens, and is grown in grass and in rockeries and window boxes. One could go on and on . . .

You don't see a wide range of fritillaries grown in British domestic gardens, possibly because they are not perhaps so easy to raise as snowdrops, possibly because they are simply not fashionable at the moment. There are hundreds of them, but only two are reasonably well known. *Fritilaria meleagris*, the snakeshead fritillary, with its strange shaped and spotted bell flower is a native British plant and many people find room for the species and some of its named varieties, such as 'Alba' and 'Aphrodite'. Snakeshead is perhaps an unfortunate name – Gerard the famous English herbalist, writing in the seventeenth century, called it the 'chequered daffodil', or the 'ginny hen fowl', which sounds much more acceptable and describes the odd chequerboard pattern of the flower just as well.

The biggest and boldest member of the clan is *Fritillaria imperialis*, the Crown Imperial, which can grow up to a metre tall, on a stem surrounded by glossy lanceolate whorled leaves – at the very top of the stem is a sort of afro hair-do of leaves, below which hang, face down, a cluster of tulip-like flowers which can be yellow or red, or shades in between.

Fritillaria imperialis is a plant around which legends have been spun. It comes originally from Persia, Afghanistan, Turkey or the Himalayas, and gained the title imperialis – imperial – because it grew at one time in the Imperial garden in Vienna. Christian legend has it that the flower refused to bow its head at the Crucifixion – thereafter it blushed and bowed its head at its presumption and always had a tear in its eye. If you turn up a head of the flower and look inside, sure enough, there is what looks like a tear. The Persian story is that the tear is there because the flower weeps for a Persian princess who was wrongly accused by her husband of infidelity.

The Crown Imperial also has a most peculiar musky scent, which some people say reminds them of foxes. On a recent trip to Holland, I was assured by several Dutch gardeners that the smell of the Crown Imperial will keep away mice and moles.

Les Bretherton, who gardens nine hundred feet up from Shrewsbury, facing Wenlock Edge, has the finest display of the yellow-flowered *Fritillaria imperialis* I've ever seen – he thinks they may be 'Lutea', but he's not sure. Six years ago, he put just ten bulbs in a circular bed, about two metres across, within his lawn and now, in April, they put up what looks like a metre-high green shrub, topped

by dozens of bright yellow flowers. Les saw, on a documentary programme on television about Yugoslavia, Crown Imperials growing by a rocky roadside in full sun, so he put his bulbs down in the sunniest spot in his garden, ignoring all that textbook advice about partial shade. He dug in plenty of well-rotted manure, scattered Growmore and put the bulbs in quite deep – about twenty centimetres, he reckons – and that seems to have done the trick. He says you have to be untidy – after the flowers have gone, the foliage is a long time a-dying, but you have to put up with that until the end of June or even the beginning of July, when the foliage has died down enough for you to be able to tug it free, gently, from the bulbs down below. He has a gnarled and twisted holly root 'sculpture' in the bed, permanently, so that there is something to look at for the rest of the year. All very unorthodox, but it works, quite beautifully.

In early May, in one of my local parks in Oldham, they still celebrate Tulip Sunday, when folk are encouraged to stroll around the park, listening to a brass band and enjoying the massed displays of brilliantly coloured giant tulips. After the display is over and the tulips

A crowded spring border, from which you can disentangle tulips, a variegated iris, honesty, saxifrage and Crown Imperials.

Parrot tulips and pansies on parade. Jack Tomlins' spring display.

have finished flowering, each bulb has to be unearthed, carefully dried off, then stored until it is replanted again in late autumn.

The average gardener has neither the time nor the space for such extravagance, but many people do love tulips and find room for a few, perhaps as focal points within a mixed border, or as part of a Spring bedding display – by far and away the most popular combination is that of tall, late, tulips, red or sometimes white, surging up boldly through a cloud of blue forget-me-nots. When that latter display is finished, you pull up the forget-me-nots, shaking them over the bed as you do so. They will thus reseed themselves, while the plants you have pulled up can go on the compost heap.

Although there is a theory that late tulips will last in the ground if you initially plant them quite deeply, most, although not all, *Garden Club* members are convinced that late spring tulips are happier if they are lifted, dried and replanted later. The best thing to do is to clean them up and strip off the yellowed foliage when they have dried off, then store them in a frost-free place until late October or early November when they can go back in the ground, although one gardener in

Swansea told me that one year he forgot to replant in October, hastily heeled them in a spare patch of ground at Christmas time and the following spring got the best display he had ever had.

A wider view of Jack Tomlins' spring garden.

Some people plant their tulips in pots, sunk flush with the ground, so that then they come to take them up again, they don't have to probe about with a fork or spade to find them, possibly disturbing other plants or shrubs in the process.

Tulips are a huge tribe, classified into sixteen divisions and I have been talking so far only about the late flowering hybrids, the two-foot monsters with huge flowers, such as the so-called Darwin hybrids or Cottage tulips. If you included early species tulips like the tiny cream-yellow *Tulipa biflora*, which can flower in a south-facing rock garden as early in March, or the lilac *Tulipa pulchella*, which can flower in a cool greenhouse in February, and worked your way through the *kaufman-niana* hybrids, the *fosteriana* hybrids, the *greigii* bybrids and so on, you could have tulips of one sort or another in bloom in different garden situations, from February to early June.

Several of the early flowering tulips, some of the species and certainly all of the kaufmanniana hybrids, have the added advantage that they can be left in the ground. *Tulipa tarda* is probably the most popular of the leave-in-ground miniature species: it has a rosette of leaves, and wonderful white flowers which open to yellow when the sun comes out.

Spring Bedding

*G*arden Club followers, like gardeners everywhere, divide into two schools of thought about bedding schemes – some don't like them at all, partly perhaps because they are too much trouble to arrange and rearrange each year, partly because they go against the 'natural' feel they prefer in their garden. The majority love to mark the spring and summer seasons with bedding.

I saw many examples of spring bedding during the course of my visits to the gardens of Club members. Already mentioned is the mix of tulips and forget-me-nots. One or two people came up with more sophisticated versions of this popular combination – for example, white and yellow tulips among a sea of pure white winter-flowering pansies. Jack Tomlins had white tulips too, set in a superb display of mixed coloured pansies, mainly whites, blues and yellows. He grows the pansies in his tiny two and a half by two metre greenhouse, then hardens them off in a cold frame before putting them out in the garden in early spring. There are now so many colour combination and variation of winter-flowering pansies that you are spoilt for choice, and could experiment for a lifetime without reaching the end of the range.

Elsewhere, I noted *greigii* tulips – these particular ones had red and yellow striped flowers – surrounded by blue muscari, or grape hyacinths. Daffodils, either white or golden, also go well with blue muscari. There was one particularly memorable show *Narcissus* 'February Gold' (flowering in March, as usual), with violet-blue *Anemone blanda* around them.

The traditional floral combination for spring bedding is tulips with wallflowers. The wallflower (*Cheiranthus cheiri*) is grown as if it was a biennial – sown outdoors in early summer, then transplanted into the chosen ground in autumn. The taproot is broken when you transplant, and once it is in its flowering position, you pinch out the top, or growing point, all of which helps to make it bushier and more floriferous come springtime. Again, as with the pansies, the choice of wallflowers these days is huge and bewildering. I picked up two useful pieces of advice – first, make sure that the contrast in size between tulip and wallflower is not too stark. There are dwarf forms of wallflower and they can look very odd when they nestle at the foot of giant tulips. Next, not all forms of wallflower are fragrant and since the scent of them can be so wonderful, it would be a pity if you missed out by unwittingly buying a variety that was not scented.

Wallflowers are not really biennials, but perennials that don't last too well, if that makes sense. I mention this because one thrifty gardener told me that he simply left his wallflowers each year and so far they had come up two years running. They had, and they do, but they soon become bedraggled and die out.

Containers

Container gardening can be, and very often is, a way of planting out spring bedding (followed by summer bedding) without using too much space. Many people who don't have a garden at all can get a partial cure for their affliction by using containers in a back yard, a patio, a window-sill or even on a roof. Even if you do have a garden, then you might still want to use containers to provide focal points, ring the seasonal changes round the front door step, soften the edges of a path or grow plants that your garden soil doesn't approve of.

You can tell that container gardening has become very popular over the last twenty years or so, because the price of choice containers, such as old stone troughs and sinks, big old-fashioned chimney pots and genuine old wooden barrels has gone through the roof and if you want that sort of thing, you now have to go for reproductions made from plastic or re-constituted stone. An ingenious gardener in Suffolk bought plastic containers, painted them ivory and then, when the paint was still tacky, scattered sand on them to give a convincing imitation of stone.

There are nice, not too expensive, things about – Chinese or Taiwanese glazed and decorated pots, terracotta pots of various degrees of sophistication, some quite plain, others based on Italian or French designs. Do make sure that the type you go for is frostproof and do keep the receipt. The degree of resistance to frost depends on the type of clay used in the pot – and this is something you cannot test when you actually buy. I met several people who had bought allegedly

A dead washing-machine becomes a container in Jack Tomlins' backyard.

frostproof pots, had them disintegrate the following Spring, then gone back to the garden centre and got their money back or a replacement. One pottery, at Whychford, in Warwickshire, does actually offer a ten-year guarantee against frost damage on its terracotta pots – the date of manufacture is stamped on the pot. They claim to have had fewer than a dozen pots returned over the last eight years.

If you use your imagination, there are all sorts of alternatives to the garden centre repertoire. *Garden Club* members have been spotted using, for example, the pedestal from a wash-basin, an old-style throne toilet bowl, a rusted up wheelbarrow and even the stainless steel drum from a dead washing machine, set horizontally on the bracket which once held it at the back of the machine. At a school in Leicester, where the children had put together a wildlife garden on the roof, they had used old school desks, large empty paint tins and even car tyres, laid on the ground with black polythene spread over then. Purists might argue that objects such as that are too ugly, but once the plants within had grown and had been encouraged to drape over the containers, it didn't seem to matter.

Whatever you use, the basic principles remain the same – your container should be able to withstand frost, and should be able to hold enough compost to sustain the plants. You will have to water a great deal, for plants in containers tend to dry out quickly – you may have to liquid feed as well, although there are now many helpful products on

A roof garden in an urban school in Leicester.

the market such as delayed action granular feeds. There should be drainage holes in the bottom of all containers, so you may have to drill holes in, say, wooden barrels or paint tins. If you use a polythene sheet base, as the children in Leicester did with their tyres, or as you may want to do with a hanging basket, it must be perforated so that

Home-made containers on the Leicester school roof.

water can get away. Containers which sit flat on the ground should be raised slightly, on bricks, so that the drainage holes can drain effectively. It also helps to put broken crocks at the bottom of the containers.

A large container, full of plants and compost will be very heavy and you may find that you cannot move it. Sometimes the answer is to put a container within a container – one of those metre-high chimney pots, for example, could have a plantpot or wire mesh basket inside it. If you are venturing up on to a flat roof, remember that a cubic metre of compost weighs a tonne and if your ceiling isn't strong enough, you may find your roof garden on your kitchen floor one morning.

Flowers for spring display could include many of the bulbs mentioned so far – snowdrops, crocuses, hyacinths, daffodils and tulips. The question of scale is important and clearly you would want to go for the smaller daffodils and tulips in smaller containers. Other flowers you might like to consider would be polyanthus, double daisies, dwarf versions of forget-me-nots and wallflowers, as well as winter-flowering pansies and winter-flowering heathers. Evergreens, such as the smaller-leaved ivies, and dwarf conifers can help to set off the flowers. It is also worth thinking of evergreens permanently in containers of their own – you can move them about throughout the year, to wherever you think they look most effective. One *Garden Club* gardener had a display, covering a large paved area, made up entirely of evergreens and dwarf conifers and it looked quite wonderful – many conifers do change colour through the seasons.

Window-boxes are a special case, and need planning and planting carefully. I met one gardener who had been on the point of fixing large, heavy window-boxes on the front of his house, when he realized that his windows opened outwards – if he had put the boxes up, he wouldn't have been able to open his windows all year. The boxes went on the ground instead. The timber for window-boxes should be treated with a wood preservative (preferably a type that doesn't harm plants) and most gardeners then line the boxes with black polythene before filling with compost and planting – don't forget to perforate the polythene above the drainage holes before the first trowel full of compost goes in. Some people prefer to put plant pots in a window-box, rather than filling the whole trough with compost. If you do that – containers within a container again – it certainly means that it is easier to change things round when spring is over and you have to start thinking of summer planting.

Hanging baskets tend to be used for summer schemes only, which is a shame, because there is no reason why they shouldn't brighten up the winter and spring. The supports for baskets should be strong and firmly fixed – it is surprising how heavy a recently watered basket full of compost and plants can be.

Dwarf and pygmy conifers can make a wonderful display in containers.

The basket will need some form of lining, to keep the compost from dribbling out, and to retain moisture. The problem is complicated by the fact that you will want to plant up the basket gradually, layer by layer, with plants emerging from the sides of the container. The classic mistake is to line the basket with black polythene, right up to the rim, then just· plant up the top – the result looks awful and you can spend the whole season looking up at a shiny black plastic bulge with a froth of colour on top.

Sphagnum moss was the classic lining material, recommended in all the gardening books. It is ideal, since it is moisture retentive, looks natural and lends itself to layered planting. The trouble is that sphagnum moss is difficult to get hold of, unless you are prepared to pay the ridiculous prices which garden centres charge. There are shaped and side-slit fibre liners which are not so expensive, but most *Garden Club* members had worked out other solutions to the problem. One man had bought a single fibre liner, then cut out similar liners in polythene, using the original as a template. Another had experimented with astroturf, which he had bought for next to nothing as offcuts: the original acid green colour eventually faded and looked quite presentable. In other baskets he had tried bits of old carpet underlay and finally he had a couple of examples with a polythene disk at the bottom of each basket, with the subsequent layers built up, bird's nest fashion, with horsehair from an abandoned mattress. This same enterprising individual always bought tomato growbags when they were out of season and on offer cheap at the garden centre and used the compost from those for his hanging baskets.

Jack Tomlins, from Shrewsbury, a cost-conscious but meticulous gardener, had a couple of valuable bits of advice for hanging basket work. He always wraps the plants he is inserting into the sides of his basket in a tube of stiff paper, so the delicate plants do not get damaged as they are squeezed between the wires, and he replaces the usual chains which suspend the baskets with stiff wire, again so that the plants do not get damaged by flopping chains when they are being placed in the top of the basket.

Alpines in troughs

Alpine flowers, grown outdoors, are one of the glories of spring and early summer in some British gardens and one of the most popular ways of growing alpines is in containers. The late Clarence Elliot and his son Joe, both commercial nurserymen specializing largely in alpine plants, were largely responsible for the popularity of growing alpines in sinks and troughs. They were able to collect a whole variety of old stone receptacles, then just falling out of use in the countryside – stone sinks, pig, cattle and horse drinking troughs, pump troughs, pig-salting sinks and one startling example of a stone Saxon coffin. Yesterday's countryside has become treasure trove for today's gardener and reproductions – or substitutes – have to be found.

Up in Grimsby, there is a very keen and enthusiastic branch of the Alpine Garden Society and one of their members, Mike Jerem, has in

Going native

Finally, one should not forget some of the British native flowers, brought in to our gardens from meadows, woodland and hedgerow.

Les Bretherton, in the hills outside Shrewsbury, has a wild flower meadow, full of British native plants. When *Garden Club* visited him, in early spring, it was dotted with primroses, cowslips, oxlips, campion and wild violets. Later, buttercups, greater celandine, yarrow and horseshoe vetch, among other gems, make their appearance and the sequence goes on into late summer, with harebells, field scabious, salad burnet and so on – all in all a wholly delightful catalogue of British wild meadow plants. Some of them – buttercups, red clover, foxgloves, herb robert – have appeared naturally, but the rest of the meadow has been carefully planted up, to give the appearance of 'nature'.

What Les Bretherton did was to raise many of these plants from seed, then when they had reached a healthy size, plant them in specially carved out patches in the grass, just to give them a start in life – if he had simply sown seed in the grass, the plants would never have been able to compete with the grass. He had a stroke of luck with his primroses – he put the seeds in a sealed jam jar, left it in a cold porch and forgot about it. The next time he looked, dozens of the seeds had germinated and sprung radicles, or little roots. He sowed them in a seed tray and dozens of them came up and developed – they were eventually hardened off and planted out. Nowadays he collects seeds and raises it in the conventional manner.

Meandering paths are mown and maintained through the grass, but apart from that, the meadow is allowed to grow and go its own way all through the season, until September – by then it is, in Les's words, 'bonnet-high on the westward side' and has to be cut down with a scythe or a large strimmer. The moral of all this is that you can't really begin to contemplate a wild meadow unless you have a fairly large area to set aside for the purpose.

A couple in Surbiton had added to their existing land by purchasing an old allotment area at the bottom of their garden for their mini-meadow. Wild flowers don't want rich soil, in fact they prefer poor soils, so the first piece of advice to anyone trying to create a meadow from existing ground is to scrape off the top ten centimetres of soil to begin with. Three years on and the Surbiton gardeners found their meadow does need careful managing – some grasses and daisies were overwhelming other plants and tending to flop over and make a mess. They were being gradually weeded out. Poppies, after a splendid show in the first year, all but died out over the following years, choked by the grasses. They had reached a compromise with their mowing, cutting the flowers and the grasses around them, by hand as the plants finished flowering and doing a final machine cut in October. If you cut everything after the spring display, you will lose all your summer flowers. If you leave the cut until autumn, it will be a big job, as Les Bretherton has already found.

A wildlife garden

You have to be courageous and very patient, though, to achieve the sort of wild-life garden which Mary Manning has built up over the years, front and back of her home in Norwich. She determined, long before anyone thought it was fashionable, that she would have a 'naturally balanced' garden, be full of wild plants and wild life: she set her face against any pesticides or garden chemicals.

As you wander through her garden, you realize that every plant has its purpose in her scheme of things – red valerian, fumitory, lavender and scabious attract the bees; nettles encourage tortoiseshell and peacock butterflies to lay eggs, while garlic mustard attracts orange-tip butterflies. Parsley is allowed to grow on to its second year to flower, to bring in hoverflies – and the hoverflies (and the wasps and ladybirds) eat greenfly. Hedges provide a habitat for thrushes and blackbirds – and they keep the slugs and the snails down. You have to be, she says, 'a bit untidy' – ladybirds hibernate in the detritus at the bottom of the box hedge, so you don't sweep up there until the spring. Newts from her various small ponds hibernate in the borders round the ponds, so she doesn't turn them over in the autumn, but waits for spring. Mary is immensely knowledgeable about all this complex ecology and keeps records of her insects, birds and wildlife – she logs the flowering of her garden on specific days each year, including a register of all the flowers in bloom in the garden on Christmas Day – the count has varied over the years from a dozen to over sixty different plants. Mary claims that she is still learning and experimenting, for example, with different ways of collecting seed and raising more plants. It might

sound as if nature is being allowed to run riot, but in fact everything is kept under careful control and besides being a fascinating place to sit and watch things going on, her garden actually looks – and is – pretty and cared for.

Spring in Mary Manning's garden in Norwich – tulips, honesty, hedge garlic and a flowering crab-apple.

Spring flowering shrubs

There cannot have been a single programme in the whole of *Garden Club*'s run which has not featured shrubs: they are the most important architectural features you can have in the garden, defining edges, backing borders, dividing up the territory, or planted as single specimens to be admired.

There can be a minor problem in seeing a shrub in magnificent full flower in a television programme or as a colour picture in a glossy catalogue and that is that you may be carried away by its beauty, rush out and buy one – and then find that it is really rather dull, apart from its brief flowering period. You should consider then, not just flower, but foliage, shape and potential size and general all year round suitability within the scheme of things in your garden. It pays, too, to listen to what is said about the plant, or read the small print in that catalogue – do you have the right sort of soil? Can you provide the protection that some shrubs need? Will it need pruning?

Several of the gardeners featured in the programmes adopted the sensible plan of keeping a newly acquired shrub in its container (repotting into a large container if the plant was already getting too big for its boots) and putting it in the garden for a whole season, moving it from place to place to find a really appropriate spot, watching how it behaved through the seasons. A couple in Shropshire had the delightful idea of creating what they called a 'friends' corner' in their garden – gardeners do tend to swap plants and here the scheme was to raise the shrubs which had been received as presents in this special patch, keeping an eye on them through a year or more, before putting them out in a selected spot in the garden proper.

Almost everyone picked up ideas on how to use shrubs by visiting other gardens regularly, at different times of the year – local gardens and parks to see the sort of things that did well in their area, famous gardens, perhaps further afield, to look for inspiration and experimentation. Jean Rawlinson, whose magnificent garden in Maghull, near Southport, has already been mentioned, makes a regular pilgrimage to Bodnant Garden, in North Wales, and her choice of shrubs, particularly rhododendrons and azaleas, is very much influenced by what she sees there. She noticed, for example, that Martin Puddle, the latest in a long dynasty of the family to be Head Gardener at Bodnant, always planted early rhododendrons, likely to be affected by frosts, in places where the sun did not get at the flowers until they had had time to unfreeze – it is the sun's rays on frozen blossom, not the frost, which does most damage. The answer is, then, to plant on the west side of the house, so that the sun does not reach the flowers until midday or after.

The range of rhododendrons available to the gardener is huge and although the majority of them would be considered to be spring flowering, if you pick your way through the repertoire, you could have flowers from late winter (there is a rhododendron called 'Christmas Cheer', which the Victorians used to force for Christmas Day, but which can be seen flowering in the open, in the south, in early January) to mid-summer.

Rhododendrons can range in size from ground-hugging plants

Jean Rawlinson's
azalea 'Irene
Koster'.

Cline Gardens, in Swansea – the sort of place where amateur gardeners go to learn.

which can get up to thirty-three metres in this country – decided it had to go, in spite of vociferous family opposition. It had roots all over the garden and took him and a friend the best part of a week's hard labour to cut down and dig up. His wife and grown-up children are still resentful, especially when they look at the family photograph album.

You only have to look around you to see example of much worse mistakes – trees planted too near the house, so that their roots are cracking drains and even foundations, while their branches thrash bedroom windows and the falling leaves of autumn block the guttering and the drains. Trees planted in front of the house, in a south-facing garden, so that now the front door and living room face darkness at noon. That hedge of Leyland cypress that isn't being kept in check and is growing a metre a year (ten centimetres a *week* in July!), and could eventually be a forest belt thirty metres high. All those Monkey Puzzle trees – tiny little things a couple of yards from the front door – that will grow to demoniacally ugly bristly monsters towering above the house.

Then there are the less dramatic errors – one couple in South Wales had planted two trees quite close together when they moved into their house thirty-odd years ago. There was a *Halesia monticola* – the fairy bell tree, or snowdrop tree – next to the neighbour's fence and in front of that a small flowering cherry. Thirty years on and the cherry had developed into a tubby-trunked tall, unattractive tree, flowering briefly and poorly in spring and doing nothing much but look ugly for the rest of the year – except that it completely obscured the view of the Halesia, which, the neighbour reported gratefully, looked wonderful hanging over her garden.

Take due warning from these examples then, and make sure you pick a tree, or trees that will fit in with your garden plan without causing trouble later on – and plant it where it will do no harm to your or your neighbour's property.

Here are some of the well-behaved, more interesting spring-flowering trees which I have seen on my Garden Club travels.

There is a nursery in Southport which has a small area set aside for plants which have lost their labels, or are damaged in some way – they call it the 'casualty department' and there are bargains to be had there if you are prepared to gamble. Jean Rawlinson bought an anonymous, bedraggled plant there, simply because she liked the look of the foliage – and it turned out to be *Halesia monticola*, the same 'snowdrop tree' which had been inadvertently hidden away in the Swansea

A flowering crab-apple – ths one is *Malus* 'Floribunda' – can be good value throughout the year.

garden. The Halesia is a beautiful deciduous large shrub or small tree for the average garden. It is covered in white flowers in May and develops curious four-sided fruits, looking rather like vandalized cigars, later on. There is a very similar species, called *Halesia carolina*, which if anything is slightly smaller. Both are named after Dr Stephen Hales, who was an English scientist back in the eighteenth century, although they both originate from Northern America. I mention this because there is another pronunciation divide here – knowledgeable plantsmen say 'Hales-eeya' while the rest of us say 'Hale-eesya'.

The name *Prunus* covers a huge and bewildering list of orna-mental plums, peaches, almonds and cherries, most of them spring flowering. We are all familiar with the brief, exhilarating glory of the white and pink blossom of these trees, for they are widely planted in public places. It pays to watch, though, what happens after flowering – and in a large number of cases, the answer is, not very much. Among *Garden Club* members the most popular choices would seem to be

Prunus 'Accolade', which has rich bunches of semi-double pink flowers in April, and retains its graceful shape throughout the year; *Prunus* 'Amanogawa', which is tall, slender and pencil thin, like a Lombardy poplar, has whitish pink, slightly scented flowers; *Prunus* 'Tai-haku', which has the largest white flowers of all and Cheal's weeping cherry, which weeps in the approved fashion and has double rose-pink flowers.

Flowering crab apples can be spectacular in spring too – with the added bonus of brightly coloured fruits in autumn. *Malus* 'Golden Hornet' has white flowers in spring and yellow fruits which can last through to Christmas and beyond: *Malus* 'John Downie' has white spring flowers too, and gives a generous supply of scarlet fruit, from which several *Garden Club* members make crab-apple jelly. Roy Lancaster's favourite ornamental crab is *Malus transitoria*, which flowers white in late spring, then produces pea-sized yellow fruits in autumn. You will have to search for this one, since it is not widely available, but there are specialist nurseries which stock it.

After apples, pears, or rather, just one ornamental pear which is very much a favourite among the *Garden Club* cognoscenti. This is *Pyrus salicifolia* 'Pendula', the willow-leaved pear, which, as its common name suggests, has long, narrow silver grey leaves, which sway sensuously in the wind, and white flowers which add to its attractiveness in April. This plant does tend to grow into a sort of impenetrable mound, and will need careful thinning out from time to time. The trick here is to penetrate the mound to get to the trunk, then from there work outwards and cut away all the dead inside branches.

During the course of both years of *Garden Club* , one bit of tree care – or rather, lack of care – cropped up time and time again. Most trees have a leader – the branch or shoot which thrusts vertically upwards as a continuation of the main trunk. Often, trees develop two competing leaders. When that happens, it is best to select the stronger of the two, and cut the other one out, otherwise the tree might eventually lose its shape and strength. It is much easier to perform this operation when the tree is comparatively small – you can do the job with secateurs rather than a saw.

Vegetables

There is an extraordinary garden at Villandry, Indre-et-Loire, France, part of which is laid out as what the French call a 'potager' – a kitchen garden would be a wholly inadequate translation of what goes on here, for the vegetables are planted out in nine squares, each outlined in dwarf box, for purely decorative effect. In May, this vegetable 'bedding' is pulled up, thrown away, and another, later season display of vegetables put in its place. Until I saw Villandry, it had never occurred to me how beautiful vegetables can look.

You can see the same sort of beauty, I now appreciate, in the work of vegetable gardeners in Britain, who grow a large selection of traditional vegetables, often in fierce but friendly competition with one another. When show-time comes round, usually in September or October, you see the most wonderful looking vegetables you ever saw in your life. It is the most skilled form of amateur gardening we have, a national cultural treasure and we should be proud of it. Spring is by far the busiest time for the dedicated vegetable grower.

Traditional rotation theory goes something like this: Root crops (potatoes, carrots, parsnips, beetroot and exotica such as chicory, salsify and scorzonera) require the soil to be enriched with fertilizer. Brassicas (cabbages, cauliflowers, kale, sprouts, broccoli, swedes and turnips) want fertilizer and lime. Legumes (pod crops such as peas and beans), plus onions, leeks, shallots, garlic, spinach, spinach beet and celery need manure or rich compost. Further, if you grow some kinds of vegetable in the same patch for year after year, then you run the risk of a build-up of pests and diseases. That risk is decreased if you can leave a gap of a couple of years between growing the same vegetable on the same patch.

Your vegetable plot is divided up into three sections for Roots (A), Brassicas (B) and Legumes and onions etc., (C) and each section treated accordingly. In the following years, you rotate the treatment and the crops, so that the three-year cycle looks like this:

First Year	Second Year	Third Year
A. Roots	C	B
B. Brassicas	A	C
C. Legumes etc.	B	A

Marigolds and
feverfew edging
Anne Stevens'
vegetable garden in
Dorset.

Several gardeners on the series stuck to this tried and trusted cycle, which is expressed most clearly and comprehensively in the Royal Horticultural Society book, wonderfully entitled *The Vegetable Garden Displayed*, but there were those who argued that potatoes should be given a class of their own, thus turning the whole thing into a four-year rotation.

Mrs Chris Neil grows all the vegetables her family needs, all through the year, in her garden in Shropshire. She learned the craft of vegetable growing in London, where she had allotments for many years and 'picked up tips from the old boys' there. Mrs Neil goes along with the idea of a four-year rotation, including potatoes in their own bed. Surprisingly (but successfully), she puts roots and legumes together in another bed, and reserves a third bed for the allium family – onions, shallots, garlic and leeks. The fourth bed is devoted to brassicas.

Most of the reference books recommend sowing broad beans in autumn, for a crop the following year – she tried this, several times, but finally gave up because the seedlings were always chewed up by mice, or slugs. Now she sows broad beans indoors in January, puts them outside later, under cloches, until they are about ten centimetres high. She harvests and freezes her broad beans before the blackfly can get at them. She has given up on conventional podded peas, because they take so long to harvest and prepare – she now grows only mange tout or sugarsnap varieties, the ones you don't need to pod. Her summer cauliflowers always went to seed, no matter what she did, so she took to growing winter cauliflowers instead. She grows a French beetroot called 'Jersey Navet', because they take only six weeks to mature from a spring planting. Mrs Neil still experiments with different potatoes each year, encouraged by the secretary of her local allotment society, which grows over a hundred varieties of potato every year. They have a trading hut, down by the allotments, where plants can be bought and sold, or exchanged. She and her family now enjoy some of the smaller, more unusual potatoes, such as 'Pink Fir Apple' and 'Ratté', but she still thinks that the best main crop variety is 'Desirée'.

In Oxford, a gardener said that it wasn't worth growing main crop potatoes in a small garden, so he grew only 'Maris Bard', an early variety: he plants a few well-chitted tubers in succession every fortnight from April to the end of June, which gives him a supply of new potatoes from mid June to the end of September.

Other gardeners I met said, forcibly, that potatoes took up far too much room (especially in a garden, rather than an allotment) and weren't worth growing, except to 'clean up' a bed that hadn't been used for some time. One retired miner in South Wales said that he *had* grown potatoes in the 1940s, to feed his family, but nowadays, it simply wasn't worth it – he challenged anyone to run a comparative test with boiled potatoes, some grown fresh, the others from a good supermarket, and to tell the difference.

Up in North Wales, near Llandudno, the allotmenteers seen in the first series would have none of this heresy – they went off each year to a specialist supplier in the Midlands and returned with 800 kilos of seed potatoes, which were distributed among their members. Their conclusions, from several years' experience, were that you must, first of all, 'chit' your seed potatoes well, which means standing them in wooden trays in a frost-free place until they sprout shoots. This tends to be done in late January or early February. Secondly, you should choose varieties which have been proved to work in your area.

They favoured a new first early potato called 'Accent', which they planted 12 to 15 centimetres deep, 25 centimetres apart, in rows 60 centimetres apart, in late February – when they could still see snow on the neighbouring mountains! In early March, they put in another couple of earlies, one called 'Foremost', the other 'Maris Bard' – they went 10 to 13 centimetres deep, 30 centimetres apart, in rows 60 centimetres apart. These would normally be harvested at the end of June. Main-crop favourites were two red-skinned varieties – 'Desirée' and 'Romano', and they were planted 40 centimetres apart, in rows 80 centimetres apart, at the same depth as the earlies. In all cases, a little manure, or sometimes a handful of grass cuttings, were put down in the trench with the seed potatoes: as the foliage grew, the potatoes were earthed up to protect them from frost.

Of other root crops, we have had useful advice on parsnips and carrots.

Parsnips can be sown directly into the ground into drills two centimetres deep and thirty centimetres apart – we saw them going into light soils in the Midlands in late March. Parsnip seed is slow and erratic in germination and so some gardeners like to sow it quite thickly and to mix it on sowing with radish seed – the radish comes up quickly and warns you where the parsnips will be later. The radishes can be harvested when they are ready. The parsnip seedlings, when they come up, should be thinned to fifteen centimetres apart. Recommended varieties are 'Avon Resister' and 'White Gem'.

Carrots for show –
after they have
been cleaned up
and polished.

Carrots are caviare to the carrot-root fly, a devastating pest which is attracted to the scene of its crimes by the smell of the bruised foliage and tunnels into the roots. Gardeners go to extraordinary lengths to avoid disturbing carrot foliage – we saw 'Amsterdam Forcing' carrot seed being sown with a seed roller, which distributes the seed evenly in the drill, and means you shouldn't have to thin out the seedlings. Another suggestion was to cover the ground with a sheet of poly-propylene fleece, which keeps off the flying insects, but lets in light, air and moisture. The problem here was to anchor the sheet on metal hoops or glass jam jars placed on sticks, just above the ground – as we saw, this can be a tricky operation in a Welsh gale. The edges of the fleece are buried under the soil.

The old-fashioned, but effective, way of going about things to thwart the dreaded carrot-root fly is to sow thinly in the first place, so that you will not have to thin out too much later – and incorporate an insecticide, such as bromophos, into the seedbed before you sow. When you do thin, water the plants first, and get rid of the thinnings quickly and a long way away. Carrots prefer a sandy soil to burrow down in – if you are on clay or stony soil, you will have to work it really well and perhaps think of growing varieties which are short rooted, like 'Amsterdam Forcing' or 'Nantes'.

Another tip for difficult-to-germinate seed, such as parsnip and carrot, is to germinate them indoors on moist, absorbent paper, at a temperature of 21°C. The seeds will sprout tiny roots – when those roots are about five millimetre long, they are mixed in Laponite gel in a clear plastic bag – you cut a corner of the bag, and squeeze the stuff out, germinated seed and all, just as you would ice a cake. The drill is then covered with soil. Chris Neil, in Shropshire, was already using this method, but Matthew Biggs went one better, and demonstrated how to mix the seed in the gel in a clear jug. Jug and contents were kept at 21°C. You could see when the seeds had germinated and when that time arrived, you simply poured the gel and germinated seed straight from the jug into the drill.

Many people grow their vegetables on what is called the 'bed system' – we saw an example down in Cornwall, very early on in the first series of *Garden Club*. The gentleman there had created raised beds, only 1.3 metres wide and boxed in with planks. I've seen people do the same thing with old railway sleepers. He could get at the vegetables within the bed from either side, without having to tread on the soil – or he could lay a plank, resting on the edging planks, and work from that. Since his soil didn't get compacted, digging was much easier – in fact there was very little in the way of digging at all, since he tended simply to put down another layer of compost to sow into each spring. Vegetables can be sown and grown much closer together than one would see on a conventional allotment – and you harvest them earlier, and at a smaller size, than usual.

There was another variation on the same theme from Surbiton, in Surrey, where a gardener, forced to give up his allotment because of ill health, had started growing vegetables on the bed system in his garden. He had four raised beds 1.3 metres wide by 6 metres long, with narrow paths between them. One plot was given over to shallots and onions, the next to root crops, the third to beans and the fourth to brassicas. He operated a four-year rotation system. He sowed runner beans, leeks, onions, lettuce, brassicas and beetroot in his greenhouse, then put them out under cloches first in the beds until the weather was milder and in this way was able to extend his growing season.

The 'bed system' was researched, tested and developed at the National Vegetable Research Station, at Wellesbourne, in Warwickshire. The work was done initially for commercial growers, but the scientists involved were enthusiastic gardeners themselves and produced two books, explaining how their work could benefit amateurs – if you want to get to the bottom of this revolution, then you should get hold of *Know and Grow Vegetables*, by P. J. Salter, J. K. A. Bleasdale, & Others, published in paperback by the Oxford University Press in two volumes, one in 1979 and the second in 1982.

Some vegetables can't be incorporated into a rotational system, but demand a permanent home of their own – asparagus, rhubarb, globe artichokes certainly need time and room to develop undisturbed and some gardeners keep their runner beans going in the same place for years, although the experts don't approve of this.

There are some disadvantages in growing your own asparagus – the bed takes up a fair amount of room, permanently, in whatever space you have available for vegetables. You may have to wait a year or two before you can gather the crop, the cropping season is very short and for the rest of the year you must leave the plants undisturbed. Weeds, especially couch grass, can be a terrible problem. On the other hand, once the bed is established, it needs very little in the way of maintenance, and could go on cropping each season for eight to twenty years.

We were able to see the early stages of asparagus growing with a lady in Cornwall who had raised some crowns from seed given by a friend and was about to put them in their permanent bed in April. The bed had been very well prepared – it had been thoroughly cleared of all weeds, then rich garden compost and seaweed had been dug in over winter. The seaweed isn't compulsory but if you have easy, free access to the stuff, as these people had, then it can be very useful. The whole bed was covered in polythene for a couple of weeks to warm up the soil.

A shallow trench had been dug, about forty-five centimetres wide and twenty-five deep. The one-year-old crowns were planted in the trench, but on an eight centimetre ridge, so that their roots draped out and downwards. It is important that the crowns are not allowed to dry out during this planting process. They were spaced about thirty-eight centimetres apart and covered with three to five centimetres of soil. You don't harvest asparagus until the third year from seed, so for the next couple of years, all you have to do is keep an eye on the weeds, and get rid of them by hand, cut down the foliage when it yellows in autumn, mound up with another three centimetres or so of soil and top dress in late February or early March with a general fertilizer. When the magic third year comes round, you cut the asparagus spears with a sharp knife, four to five centimetres below the surface of the soil. Harvest for only four or five weeks, then resume the previous pattern of care. If all has gone well, you should be happy for several years to come.

Growing vegetables for show at County or National level is a very serious business indeed and calls for skills and experience of the very highest order. We were shown some of the secrets by a grower who competes regularly – and successfully – at the prestigious Shrewsbury Show. This was especially impressive because one of the vegetables he specialized in was the cauliflower. Anyone who can grow cauliflowers well deserves respect, for they are a very difficult and temperamental beast.

He grew his cauliflowers from seed – he preferred 'Dok Elgon', or 'All the Year Round'. He sowed his first tray full of seed in the second week in March, sowing further trays every ten days – six trays altogether, spread over sixty days. The seedlings in each tray were transferred into eight-centimetre pots ten days after they had germinated. They were grown on under glass, hardened off and planted out in the open at the end of April, in well-worked, fertile soil. Each plant was provided with a collar around the base to prevent the cabbage-root fly from laying its eggs – the seed bed was dusted with Bromophos too. The plants were fed regularly with Q4 fertilizer, and given one feed of nitro-chalk. They were sprayed with Picket, a pyrethrum-based insecticide, every fourteen days. Watering was vital – the plants should never be allowed to go short of water. The best of the bunch were selected for the Shewsbury Show, which is held at the end of August or beginning of September.

Summer

Signs

The last spring frost marks an important turning point in the gardener's year – summer has begun. As a broad general rule, so the text books say, the last frost in the south of Britain – south, that is, from a line drawn across the country from the Wash to Aberystwyth – can be expected around the 16th of May. North of that line, the date could be anything from ten to fourteen days later. The date is important, because the end of the frosts means that you can put summer bedding outside to replace the spring displays, and get to work with all those plants which thrive in summer but cannot cope with frosts. Broad general rules are useful, but it is better, every time, to consult local gardeners. *Garden Club* gardeners come up with some interesting local variations.

I have already mentioned the sky-watcher in Southport who puts his faith in the birds – when the swallows arrive over Southport, usually around the 15th May, he puts out his summer bedding. Further south, in Oxford, another gardener notes the first sound of the local cuckoo – the 12th of April seems to be the date – and puts her bedding out a month later. Many gardeners become addicted to weather forecasts on local radio or television at the end of May or the beginning of June, for no matter which date you decide upon action, you could be caught out by a wickedly late frost. If the frost is forecast, then plants will need protection for the night.

Summer bedding

Raising summer bedding plants is a time consuming, risky business, so many people don't bother – they buy them from the garden centre already growing in trays, plugs or pots. If you are a member of a gardening club or an allotment society, you may well be able to buy them considerably more cheaply via the organization, or you may find that one or two members of the group will grow them and sell them to the others. We saw a fine example of this in Ballymena, Northern Ireland, where one gardener, who relished the challenge, was growing plants for friends and neighbours.

Seeds for summer display are sown, under glass, or some sort of cover. Different types of plant are sown at slightly different times:

antirrhinums and begonias can be sown in January or February; petu-nias, salvias and lobelias from February to March; ageratums, dahlias and mesembryanthemums in March, and African and French mar-igolds, asters and nicotianas from March to April. It makes sense to stagger the sowings anyway, otherwise, if the seedlings all develop at the same time, the workload of pricking out or transplanting can be overwhelming.

A favourite bedding annual – an unknown sport from a viola in an Oxford garden.

In Ballymena, we saw how the seeds were sown – seed compost was put into trays, to within a centimetre or so of the top, the compost was then gently firmed flat with a wooden presser and then watered from a can with a fine rose. Some seeds are very fine and you have to be careful that you spread the seed evenly, but not too thickly – some people mix such seed with fine sand before sowing, which helps to spread them out. The seed of *Begonia semperflorens* is actually worth more than its weight in gold, so you get a tiny amount of near invisible dust in the packet and it needs careful handling to make sure you get your money's worth. Larger seed, such as marigolds or ageratum are much easier to spread out. They will need covering with a thin screen

You need a steady hand and a lot of patience when it comes to pricking out, but Albert Bird of Swansea has had years of practice.

of compost, or, as seen in Northern Ireland, with a scattering of vermiculite.

In Ballymena, both types of seed were covered, after sowing, with sheets of glass, then newspaper, and put into a propagator, where they were kept warm and moist until they germinated. This can happen very quickly with some seeds – the ones we saw, of ageratum, were through in three days, others take longer. You don't need a propagator – a gardener in Shropshire used a special electrically warmed plate, while a lady in Oxfordshire, living and working in extremely limited space on board a canal boat, used a fan heater. Many people use the airing cupboard.

It is crucial, once the seeds are through, that you take them out of the warmth and grow them on in cool conditions, otherwise the plants become long, thin and drawn out and collapse in a heap when you water them. It is also essential to be scrupulously clean, sterilizing all containers before you use them and keeping all working surfaces tidy.

Once the first leaves, the seed leaves, or cotyledons, are up, it is time to prick out – this is the part that enthusiasts love and lesser mortals find very tedious. More trays are prepared, then the seedlings are lifted out of the seed trays one by one, and replanted, regularly spaced, into the new containers. The seedlings are lifted with the help

of a small stick – a dibber, a pencil or even one of those wooden-notched spoons you get with some ice-cream tubs. They must be picked up by the seed leaves, to avoid damage to the true leaves and you can expect to get about forty seedlings in a standard sized tray. They are grown on, under cover, until it is time to put them outside.

Even then, you must be careful. You have to accustom the young plants to outside conditions by hardening them off, which means leaving them outside on reasonable days, but bringing them in again at night. If you have a cold frame, the job is much easier.

Many people raise perennial plants – delphiniums, lupins, phlox, heleniums, hemerocallis, scabious, nepeta, and heucheras and the like – from seed, using the same methods as those described above, although you can sow the seed outdoors in a prepared bed in late spring, or buy plants and eventually propagate them by division.

If everything has gone according to plan with your sowing of bedding plants, you will move them to their permanent outside positions after that last frost. We saw some memorable summer displays, well worth the time and the trouble taken. Jack Tomlins, in Shrewsbury, transformed his front garden by replacing his spring bedding of bulbs and winter-flowering pansies with a dazzling display of ageratum, verbena, multiflora begonias, impatiens (Busy Lizzies), and lobelia.

Boxes, baskets and containers

Many people put out their summer plants in containers, rather than in the ground. Jane Fanner-Hoskin is the lady on the canal boat – a beautifully converted working boat, dating from 1906, and now moored just outside Oxford. Her summer bedding is in wooden troughs on the roof of the boat and on the bankside, and in hanging baskets on the side of the vessel. Many gardeners like to mix up the colours of summer bedding in riotous confusion, but Jane prefers to match the colours of the flowers with the colours of the painted boxes. The recipe is well worth a look:

Yellow boxes contain *Chrysanthemum paludosum, Chrysanthemum* 'Polar Star', *Marigold* 'Solar Gold', *Nasturtium* 'Whirlybird Gold', *Thunbergia alata* 'Susie' (Black-eyed Susan), and *Petunia F1 Hybrid* 'White Magic'.
Red Boxes included *Adonis aestivalis* (Pheasant's Eye). *Geranium F1*

Hybrid 'Sensation Scarlet', *Linum grandiflorum* 'Bright Eyes', *Nasturtium* 'Empress of India', *Amaranthus caudatus* (Love Lies Bleeding) and *Petunia grandiflora* 'Red Express'.

Blue boxes were planted up with *Nemophila maculata* '5 Spot', *Ageratum* 'Blue Mink', *Lobelia* 'Cambridge Blue', Pansy 'St Lucia', *Nolana* 'Blue Bird' and, for its silver foliage, which sets off the blue, *Cineraria maritima* 'Silver Dust'.

Jane's hanging baskets were made up largely of pink flowers – *Impatiens* 'Super Elfin Blush', *Petunia grandiflora* 'Pink', *Verbena* 'Amour Light Pink', *Lobelia* 'Cascade Mixed', *Nepeta mussinii* and three varieties of fuchsia.

All plants in containers have to be watered twice a day – Jane also feeds the plants with a liquid fertilizer – in her case Phostrogen – once a week.

Jack Tomlins has hanging baskets, as well as his front garden bedding display. These are rather special. Anyone who has holidayed abroad, especially in Switzerland, Austria or the Alsace region of

Left: Summer bedding combines quite beautifully with traditionally painted canalware.

Right: Container plants dry out quickly and need frequent watering. Jane's son sometimes lends a hand.

Jack Tomlins has
trained one of his
pink geraniums as a
standard.

France, will have been struck by the rich and seemingly endlessly flowering displays of geraniums in window-boxes and other containers. Jack was struck too – and brought some cuttings home. He doesn't know the specific names of his plants, but refers to them simply as red, white and pink. They have been a regular part of his repertoire for several years now – he takes cuttings in late summer and keeps them in five-centimetre pots in his greenhouse from November to January, when they move up into eight-centimetre pots. He plants up his baskets in March, but keeps them standing on plant pots under polythene cover outside before hanging them up in mid June. They are watered well, fed with a high nitrogen fertilizer for foliage, changing to high potash for the flowers.

An Oxfordshire gardener specialized in hanging globes, which he made by completing two thirty-five-centimetre hanging baskets, filled with compost and plants, each with a perforated tube, funnel-shaped at the top, in the centre and flush with the top of the compost. The funnel in one basket was put in upside down, with a funnel looking down: when this basket was filled, a wire mesh was fastened across the top. In one swift and courageous move, this basket is turned upside down and put on top of the other and both wired together to make the globe. The mysterious business with the tubes makes watering easier and more efficient – you can actually buy these tubes specially made, but the Oxfordshire gardener had seen the originals at the Chelsea Flower Show and borrowed the idea, making his own from bits of plastic drainpipe. The whole ensemble was planted up with about a hundred red and white bedding begonias. If you attempt this minor miracle yourself, take warning and make sure the support for the globe is very strong, for the whole ensemble is very heavy and took two people to lift it from the ground. This particular Oxford monster was hung in a small greenhouse – to bring it outside for filming, or any other sort of display, would have involved dismantling the whole of the front of the greenhouse.

Faint-hearted – and wealthy – gardeners can achieve the same globe effect by buying a comparatively new product called a Flower-ball, which is a complex plastic sphere with spaces for small flower pots, intersown with thin plastic tubing forming an internal watering system. Not so much fun, though.

Fuchsias and geraniums

The fuchsia is a beautiful, hugely varied flower, which is often used as part of summer bedding schemes. It is also an infinitely versatile plant and can be found performing as a hedge, a shrub, a house plant, trained as a ball, a fan or a standard, as well as in summer containers, window boxes and hanging baskets.

A retired gentleman in Southport showed how simple it is to take cuttings from a fuchsia in early Spring – he snipped off the top couple of inches of a shoot with a pair of scissors, stripped off all the leaves apart from the rolled-up cluster of new ones at the top of the shoot, then put the cutting in a small jar of water for an hour to 'have a good drink'. After that, the cutting was dipped in hormone rooting powder, then dibbled into a pot of compost with a pencil. Several cuttings can be put together into one small pot. He then made sure that he fine-sprayed the cuttings every twenty-four hours. They were sheltered in his 'greenhouse', which was actually a pensioned–off garage converted for plants by putting windows of clear corrugated plastic in the roof.

He didn't have room in his garden for cold frames, so he had built a narrow open-fronted shed, with shelves. The front could be covered up with frames of plastic if a frost threatened. What he had, in fact, was a sort of *vertical* cold frame, built himself at very little cost and taking up very little space. Within it, he could harden off his fuchsias (and many other plants).

Geraniums are also a much-loved element in summer bedding and container planting. I now step gingerly into an area of huge confusion. *Those* geraniums – the ones we use for bedding – are not really geraniums at all, but zonal pelargoniums. Geraniums are hardy plants which tend to be parked permanently in the herbaceous border. Because the general public stubbornly refuse to recognize the distinction, nurseries and garden centres have had to go along with the confusion and label both types of plant 'geranium'. There is a famous nursery, specializing almost entirely in zonal pelargoniums, which has had to give up the struggle and call itself the Vernon Geranium Nursery – they put out a brochure to explain all this, and its heading is 'Confusion! Confusion!'

The gentleman in Southport also demonstrated how to take geranium (pelargonium) cuttings, pointing out that the technique is

the same for geranium (geranium) cuttings – he cut off a five-centimetre shoot, just below a node, or joint, leaving the small leaves at the top. Again, they were dipped in the hormone rooting powder, then dibbled into pre-watered compost. The important difference between the preparation of these and the fuchsia cuttings is that geraniums will die if you overdo the water treatment – they don't need the fine spray and in fact shouldn't be watered at all, after the cuttings have been taken, for ten days.

Once you have established fuchsias or pelargoniums in your house or garden, then you keep them going by cuttings and by overwintering the plants.

Most of these exotics are brought out when all danger of frost has passed. The New Zealand cabbage tree (*Cordyline australis*) is wrapped up for the winter in netting and straw. Will Giles' Norwich garden.

Exotics and fond memories

Will Giles, who has a sheltered south-facing and sloping garden in Norwich, has evolved his own very exotic version of summer display. He has the European Fan palm (*Chamaerops humilis*), the

Part of one of Will Giles' exotic-looking herbaceous borders, including the scarlet dahlia 'Bishop of Llandaff', the yellow dahlia 'Yellow Hammer' and *Crocosmia* 'Emily McKenzie', plus a cloud of yellow *Rudbeckias*.

Chusan Palm (*Trachycarpus fortunei*) and New Zealand Cabbage trees (*Cordyline australis*), growing outdoors, within sight of his front door. They are all protected through the winter – their leaves are wrapped up together and covered with netting and straw. When summer comes round, he adds to the sub-tropical feel of the place by bringing out plants which have been kept in the conservatory over winter, either standing them in pots on his front step, or plunging them, still in their pots, into a bed at the front of the house. These include agaves, those spiny plants you see all over the Mediterranean; aeoniums, strange succulents which look like petrified roses; echeverias, yuccas and puyas. Among them, other plants, such as French lavender, flourish. It is truly hard to believe you are in Norwich.

A little further South, in Suffolk, another gardener used exotic plants, protected in a greenhouse through the winter and put out in pots in May, to give a sub-tropical throb to his garden. There is an unusual foliage plant from New Zealand, *Astelia chathamica* Silver Spear; the common coral tree, from Brazil, with its deep red, waxy flowers on arched stems and perhaps most startling of all, a Brugmansia, or

Angel's Trumpet, from Mexico, with long, drooping trumpet-shaped flowers – this one was *Brugmansia* × *insignis*, also known as *Datura suaveolens*. There were agapanthus, or African lilies, here too, in various shades of blue. In some southern gardens, you can leave these outside over winter, with some protection such as a mulch of bracken or coarse sand, but here, the crowns were lifted after the plants had died down, and kept in a dry shed, just as you would do with dahlia tubers.

There were other gardeners who had raised plants at home as fond memories of foreign holidays: invariably such plants were protected during the winter and only put outside from June to September or early October. There is an evergreen shrub called *Pittosporum tobira*, with shiny green leaves and headily scented white flowers in late spring, which can be found in all sorts of guises in Greece, Italy and Yugoslavia – sometimes a simple shrub, but often clipped as a hedge and sometimes trained as a standard tree. It actually comes from Japan. In southern parts of Britain, it can be grown outside in a sheltered spot by a warm sunny wall; further north, it is kept as a tender pot plant and taken out only when the season is kind.

There was one *Garden Club* gardener who had a plant with a poignant story attached – he and his wife had eaten loquats (*Eriobotrya japonica*) gathered from a nearby tree, at an open air restaurant in Yugoslavia, brought the seeds home and raised half a dozen plants from them. They were kept in a frost free place until June, then put outside. The plants, with huge, deeply veined leaves, dark green on top and velvety brown underneath are really rather impressive and reminded them of holiday places which they may never see again, because of the horrific disintegration of what was Yugoslavia. They have now heard, incidentally, of other British gardeners who have had similar plants for some time, whose specimens have actually flowered in especially hot summers, such as that of 1989.

The delight of cottage gardens

Many have a romanticised view of the typical English cottage garden – a quaint, picturesque cottage smothered in honeysuckle and old roses, fronted, in an unplanned and artless fashion, by homely, old fashioned flowers – Sweet Williams, hollyhocks, pinks, foxgloves and lupins and the like. (No Latin names here, of course). Somewhere in the background there will be, perhaps, an apple tree and a row of scarlet flowered runner beans.

Garden Club has visited several cottage gardens during the course of its summer season wanderings and each time I was struck by what a complicated, busy and skilled business the management of a cottage garden actually is. As Gertrude Jekyll, the great lady gardener who raised the cottage garden to an art form over a century ago, once said, 'One can hardly go into the smallest cottage garden without hearing or observing something new.'

Sonia Kinahan's garden, in a small village a mile or so from Norwich, is tiny, measuring something over seven by four metres. It is sheltered by brick walls, and full of traditional cottage garden flowers – cowslips and primrose in spring, and in summer, delphiniums, hollyhocks, violets, foxgloves and honesty, not to mention old roses. The first lesson to be learned from this repertoire is that weeding is a highly skilled procedure – you must learn to recognize the difference between weeds and desirable plants at the seedling stage – you don't want groundsel and dandelions, but you do want to preserve the self-sown foxgloves and at least some of the prolifically seeding honesty. Once you have done that, the next stage is to mulch everything (Mrs Kinahan does that with bark fibre), to conserve moisture around the plants and to smother the weeds.

Mrs Kinahan grows fruit as well, mixed in apparent glorious confusion with everything else. Not just the odd apple tree for her, though – she has greengages, a pear tree, gooseberries, raspberries, black and white currants, a fig, alpine strawberries and an edible quince (*Cydonia oblonga*) as well. And in between all that, in the summer, she grows runner beans, lettuce, outdoor tomatoes, courgettes and herbs.

Her garden is anything but 'artless' – there are some delightful and thoughtful combinations, including the pencil-shaped ornamental cherry, *Prunus* 'Amanogawa' with *Clematis alpina* 'Pamela Jackman' twining up through it and a yellow-flowered *Coronilla glauca*, through which peeped the low-growing blue-flowered *Ceanothus thyrsiflorus repens*.

Finally, the tiny garden boasts tender plants, which she grows and protects outdoors through the year – a red flowered oleander, a *Pittosporum tobira*, a passion flower and a fremontodendron. The secret of nursing the tender plants, she says, is to plant them close together, preferably near a wall, and to cover up in the worst weather with

An unusual
variegated form of
that old cottage
garden favourite,
honesty (*Linaria*
'Variegata').

anything that comes to hand – cardboard boxes for the smaller plants, bubble plastic wrappings for the stems of climbers.

There was another cottage garden, this time in Southport. Here, among the host of traditional flowers, were some which needed strict control – sweet woodruff, snow-in-summer (*Cerastium tomentosum*) and *Saxifraga × urbium* London Pride. Unless you thin these things out rigorously, they will take over the garden. When the lady inherited this small garden, it was, as she said, 'wall-to-wall grass' – now, there was no sign of a lawn and the whole thing consisted of island beds, packed with flowers, and threaded by narrow, winding paths – there were astilbes, galtonias, alstroemerias, delphiniums, foxgloves, hollyhocks, a beautiful Angel's Fishing Rod (*Dierama pulcherrima*) and many, many more. Something not immediately recognizable turned out to be *Medicago arborea*, the Moon Plant, with yellow flowers and, later, crescent shaped seed pods. When I said to the lady, innocently, that her garden seemed more sophisticated that the usual cottage garden, and perhaps not really a cottage garden at all, she seemed momentarily taken aback, then came out with the best definition of that elusive phenomenon of the cottage garden I've ever heard: 'Well, I live in a cottage and this is my garden – so it must be a cottage garden!'

Water power

There is a large and very beautiful pool within the grounds of Wakehurst Place, Kew Garden's 'place in the country' in Sussex. In summer, the dark water is covered with huge, sumptuous, water-lilies – pink, white, resting jewel-like on their floating green plates of foliage. Moorhens skitter about, leading convoys of young ones, who look like nothing more than animated balls of black fluff. From the pool, green lawns sweep up to the house, which is framed in trees. So many visitors with cameras stop for this entrancing view, that the Wakenhurst staff call it 'Kodak Corner'. We can't all have a water feature as grand as this, but can go for something a little less imposing, but no less interesting.

Tony and Marian Watts started off in a modest way, in their back garden in Norwich with a half-barrel of water, sunk flush with their lawn. They had picked up the idea from a television programme, but decided that the wooden barrel recommended was too expensive –

Autumn poolside: *Dierama pulcherrimum* (Angel's fishing rod), *Cyperus alternifolius* and *Houttuynia cordata* 'Chameleon'.

their local garden centre wanted to charge them £20. They made do with one of those half-barrel-size plastic containers, often used for summer bedding, but in this case, they didn't punch the holes in the bottom for drainage, but left it at it was. That cost £3. They filled it with water and put fifteen centimetres of mud in the bottom. They were given some bits of floating oxygenating plants by a neighbour, planted a water-rush in a basket with earth and pebbles on top in the middle of the pool, introduced tadpoles and waited to see what would happen.

The first news was not good – they came home from holiday to find their tiny pond positively foaming with what looked like green pea soup – it was algae. They didn't quite know what to do about it, but that night it rained and in a couple of days the water was clear. The moral of that is, don't panic, but wait and see if the natural balance of life in the water asserts itself. Later, they realized that the tadpoles which had graduated into frogs couldn't actually get out of their pond, so they put stones in one side to provide a kind of step ladder. They very much enjoyed the rest of the year, watching the dragonflies, damsel flies, water beetles and other creatures who were attracted to their private stretch of water.

A retired couple, both in their eighties and living in Suffolk, had much the same experience. The husband had been a builder, so he had put together something a little more ambitious – he set down three half-barrels, close together, like the ace of clubs, and set paths of flat stones in concrete round the rim. The water supply came from the flat roof of their kitchen, via a drainpipe: there was an overflow system beyond the pond that fulfilled a dual purpose – it stopped the pond overflowing uncontrollably, and produced a boggy area, where wetland plants could flourish. In the pond there was a tiny fountain, worked by a submersible pump – the sprinkler for the fountain was a perforated cone from his wife's cake-icing set.

Marion Watts saw another television programme, this time about the French artist Monet and his famous gardens at Giverny, featuring the water lilies that became one of his most memorable motifs. This inspired her and her husband Tony to set about building and stocking a more ambitious pond than their much-loved plastic half-barrel. First, they looked for the right spot in the garden – they wanted to see it from their kitchen window, but to keep it out of the way of falling autumn leaves from their neighbour's garden. There turned out to be a shrubbery in the way, but they decided to make use of some of that, because Marion wanted not only plants in the pool, but larger plants outside, which would be reflected in the water, just the sort of thing she had seen in the programme about Monet.

Tony dug out the hole where the pond was going to be – neighbours were persuaded to barrow some of the debris away in the form of free topsoil for their own gardens. The hole was five metres long by three wide, sixty centimetres deep in the middle, with a shelf which was to be fifteen centimetres or so deep, around the edges. Next a thick layer of sand was spread, and on top of that a butyl lining was laid – the cushioning layer of sand ensured that the butyl would not be cut, chafed or punctured by sharp stones. The pond was filled; then, when everything had settled, a collar of flagstones was laid around the rim of the pond and on top of the overlay of butyl.

This pond was large enough for the three types of plant which most water features should have – oxygenating plants, such as *Elodea crispa*, *Callitriche verna* (water starwort) and *Aponogeton distachyus* (water hawthorn); marginal plants, which go on the shelving in shallow water – these could include various irises, the sweet scented rush and marsh marigold; and deep water aquatics, of which the water lilies (*Nymphaea*) are the best known. The Watts found that their water lilies were very small at first, and so blanket weed tended to be a problem. A neighbour gave them some more mature plants from his own pool and they found that their larger leaves covered more water, sheltering it from the sun, and so kept the blanket weed down.

They now find they have a feature in their garden which they can enjoy the whole year through – the plants in the pond and along its margins and the wildlife which comes to call. They are now identifying different kinds of dragonfly and damsel fly, with the aid of a book, and are becoming experts on newts. The shrubs which they left near the side of the pond are reflected beautifully in the water – a red rhododendron in spring, a white philadelphus a little later and a pink lavatera in summer.

There is a further sophistication – they too have a boggy area by their pond, which they made by extending the butyl shallowly at one end, puncturing it deliberately, so that water seeps out. There is a barrier between pond and bog, which they made by creating a porous dam made up of flexible plastic mesh greenhouse shading rolled up in a kind of large sausage. They put manure in the bottom of the boggy patch, and planted astilbes and hostas and other moisture-loving plants.

There have been, of course, many other examples of water

gardening shown on *Garden Club* – like the man in Leicester who got very enthusiastic and had to be restrained by his wife from turning the whole of his back garden into a water feature. He made do with three interlocking pools, each one lower than the next, with waterfalls in between and a fountain which emerges from the hub of an old cart wheel, sunk flat in a bed of stones. He baulked at the cost of butyl and constructed the whole thing from damp course material, overlaid with builders' plastic, overlaid with PVC with nylon threads. In Suffolk, we saw an early summer 'room' of a professional garden designer's garden, which had a raised pool, built of brick, with a flat capping of stones to sit on – from that vantage point, you could admire not only the water lilies, but an ancient, greedy carp called Moby Dick.

Eddie Joynson, in Southport, got interested in gardening through keeping fish. First, he designed and built a formal patio pool for his fish, then, as he started to collect Japanese Koi carp, he began to ponder a Japanese garden, with water, gravel, stones and plants.

He got his first ideas from a calendar he saw at work – ironically, he works for an electronics firm whose main competitors are the Japanese and for some mysterious reason they had calendars, with ravishing photographs of Japanese gardens, hanging on the walls. Now, he has pools, with water flowing gently from one to another over shallow waterfalls. There are large stones by the water, set in patterns partly according to ancient Japanese rules, partly dictated by his exhaustion in shifting them about. There is a curved wooden bridge and the latest addition is a wooden tea house – he doesn't take tea there, but uses it as a garden shed to keep the lawnmower and garden tools in. In one corner, water trickles from a bamboo stand pipe (a kakeshi) down into a bowl carved in the top of a large round stone (a tsukubai) – Eddie discovered that a local carpet firm used to take delivery of oriental carpets spooled on large bore bamboo canes, so he got his material from them. He chipped and drilled out the stone bowl himself, a process which he doesn't recommend, since it takes weeks and wears out tools. The waterways and pools are surrounded by appropriate plants – an *Acer palmatum* 'Dissectum', an *Aucuba japonica*, a flowering cherry, bamboos and grasses. The whole ensemble already had a tranquil, almost timeless feel – it is a very soothing place to be. Eddie has started to find books on the subject of Japanese gardening, and specialist nurseries, and is getting more and more interested in the ideas behind it all.

If you have a naturally boggy patch in your garden, then you can

Candelabra
primulas – perfect
for boggy ground.

Some people find the Blue Himalayan Poppy (*Meconopsis betonicifolia*) difficult to get established – but it is well worth the struggle.

turn it to your advantage by incorporating lots of manure and putting in plants which like that environment. If your garden is dry, then make an area like Mr Watts did, by sinking a 'bowl' of punctured polythene, lined with upside down turves and layered with manure and kept permanently damp – a further example was found in Grimsby, with wonderful plants, like the three-foot-tall, yellow-flowered *Ligularia przewalskii*, the flame flowered *Lobelia cardinalis* and a splendid collection of Candelabra primulas, such as *P. japonica, P. florindae* and *P. beesiana. Primula seiboldii*, with its clear violet flowers and unusual notched leaves, was growing vigorously here as well. There were native plants too, including the marsh marigold (*Caltha palustris*) and the globe flower (*Trollius europaeus*). My favourite, by far, was a magnificent five-foot-high Himalayan blue poppy (*Meconopsis betonicifolia*).

Over on the other side of the same town, Grimsby, a gardener who admired bizarre and unusual plants had a bog garden on the edge of his pond, into which he had inserted, in pots, a collection of carnivorous plants, including a sundew, *Drosera rotundifolia*, a pitcher plant, *Sarracenia catesbaei* and his favourite, *Darlingtonia californica*, the cobra lily. He had failed four or five times with this last plant, but persevered and finally found that it did not enjoy the confines of a pot, and did better when allowed a free root run under pebbles. He passed some of his time during the summer, watching these plants drown, devour or otherwise destroy insects. There were other carnivorous plants, non-hardy, and on his kitchen windowsill. It had all started with his buying a simple Venus flytrap from a supermarket.

Borders

One of the truly astounding and exhilarating sights of high summer is a traditional herbaceous border – a phenomenon usually only to be found these days in the large show-place gardens such as those of the National Trust. There is a justly famous double herbaceous border at the RHS garden at Wisley, divided by the broad grassy Broadwalk and bounded by high hornbeam hedges. In July and August, the borders are filled to bursting point with clouds of phlox, waves of geraniums, golden plates of achillea and spires of hollyhocks and delphiniums and many, many more marvels. On warm summer days, there is a constant murmuring of bees, a heady mix of scents, a blaze of colour – and lots of gardeners with notebooks, twisting and craning to see the labels on the plants.

The heyday of the herbaceous border was across the turn of the century, when Gertrude Jekyll and her contempories planned out vast masterpieces, painting with flowers, grading the plants by size and colour so that they rose, from tiny border plants at the front to huge monsters at the back. Graham Stewart Thomas, one of our great contemporary gardeners and garden writers, who has recently redesigned the Wisley borders, once described a visit to Gertrude Jekyll's garden quite brilliantly: 'To see in reality those wonderful borders of graded colour was like an entry into a new world, or walking through a static rainbow.'

These marvellous creations were, however, extremely labour intensive – once the beds were dug, manured, planned and planted, the plants had to be staked and supported, dead-headed after they had flowered, then cut down at the end of the season. The following spring, established plants were divided and replanted. They took up a huge area – and left it looking bleak and uninteresting from autumn through to the following summer. Nowadays, people shun the traditional border and use herbaceous perennials in more modest schemes of mixed planting, including bulbs, shrubs and annuals. We have arrived at the mixed border.

Christina Abbott, who gardens in Knaresborough, in North Yorkshire, *has* built up a herbaceous border in her garden and it is worth travelling a long way to see. She started, she said, 'with all the plants I could afford, a spade, a fork, a strong back and a thick head.' She had a suitable sunny area at the bottom of her garden, backed by existing shrubs and trees. The hardest work came with the initial preparation, for the ground must be scrupulously weeded, thoroughly dug over, well manured and fertilized – the plants are going to be there a long time and they need all the help they can get. Back in the early 1970s, Chris's border was a comparatively modest affair, some ten metres long and two metres wide: she has gradually extended it and it now stretches across twenty-five metres and at its deepest it is eight metres from front to back.

Now, almost twenty years on, her annual plan of campaign begins in August, when the border is looking its glorious best – there isn't too much work to do, apart from dead-heading, and she has time to admire and criticize the year's display, making mental notes on what has worked and what she wants to change. In October, every-

thing is cut down and tidied up – she no longer has autumnal plants, such as Michaelmas daisies and dahlias. She lifts and divides, replans and replants in autumn. Many people would do that in the spring, but Chris has too many other things to do in the garden at that time of year. When everything is sorted out to Chris's satisfaction, she spreads a thick mulch of well-rotted manure around all the plants in the bed.

Will Giles' mixed border in late summer – acanthus, osteospermum, rudbeckia, thistles and sedums on view.

There are two ways of dividing up established herbaceous plants – you can take what are called 'Irishman's cuttings', which are simply rooted pieces prised away from the edge of the plant, or you can lift the whole thing and split it, usually by forcing it apart with two garden hand forks placed back to back. There are several reasons for division: often, herbaceous plants get thick and congested and start to rot in the centre, so you are simply preserving their health by taking the best bits from the side and discarding the rest. It is a good idea to move plants around within the border from time to time, so that the danger of picking up diseases is lessened. You also divide to increase your supply – not many people can afford to follow those elaborate planting plans which appear in the gardening books, so what they do, in Knaresborough and elsewhere, is start off in a modest way, gradually building up their stock by propagation and, most important, this – swopping healthy plants with friends and fellow enthusiasts. I should stress the word 'healthy', for it is dreadfully easy to inherit diseased plants – Chris has had nightmares in the past about phlox eelworm and the like.

Many herbaceous favourites are enthusiastic colonizers and their ambitions have to be curbed – *Alchemilla mollis*, the Lady's Mantle, has beautifully fresh foliage and lovely feathery greenish-yellow flowers, but its seeds spread wickedly. The answer is to cut it down after flowering and before seeding, usually in August – your reward will be fresh foliage before the season ends. (The vice of colonization becomes a virtue if you are growing Lady's Mantle as ground cover, rather than as part of the border.) One of Christ Abbot's favourite giants standing guard at the back of the border is the biennial Scotch thistle, *Onopordum acanthium*, which rears up to six feet or more before putting out the familiar purple flowers. Many people are terrified of this plant and struggle to keep it *out* of the garden, because it covers the ground about it with young plants, looking like spiny explosions. Chris loves it, and gives away the seedlings to neighbours.

Then there are those herbaceous plants which will not grow old gracefully, but become tough and woody and less and less attractive – the perennial wallflower, *Erysimum* 'Bowles' Mauve' (see plant of the week on page 182), is one of them and the best thing to do here when age begins to overtake it is to take cuttings in August and replace the old plant with its progeny the following spring. Penstemons, with foxglove-like flowers which can last all through summer and into autumn, are among the most popular of all the herbaceous perennials. In some gardens they will survive the winter with a covering of some sort, in colder areas you would take cuttings in August for next year's plants, or take them into the greenhouse in October. One of the more recent arrivals in the herbaceous border is the diascia, which comes from South Africa: *Diascia rigescens* has delicate pink flowers, curiously spurred at the back. This is a tender perennial and you should take cuttings in summer and cuttings from those cuttings the following spring.

I mention these few examples from among many to make the point that each and every one of the herbaceous perennials – and I have mentioned only a handful of plants from the hundreds available

– has its own personality and peculiarities and needs appropriate care to flourish.

In February, Chris Abbott scatters Growmore over the whole bed, then, as the plants grow, she stakes the larger ones – delphiniums get canes, others are supported by stick and twigs and sometimes wire mesh. The trick here is to put in the support at the right time, before the plants get too big. This timing can only come with experience – if you do it too soon, the plants will outgrow their support and flop over, if you leave it too late, you will find that they will still look trussed up and clumsily corseted when they are fully grown.

Chris has to tread delicately when she does all this work, because to extend the season in her herbaceous border she has planted narcissi and tulips with forget-me-nots. The tulips, by the way, stay where they are – she has planted them deeply, at about twenty centimetres and reckons that this does the trick. The forget-me-nots self-seed as they are gathered up, soon after flowering.

There is no getting away from the fact that all this is hard work and Chris sometimes wonders how she will be able to cope as she gets

Blue pensemons and white linums blend together beautifully.

Another border in late summer, with diascias, penstemons, polygonums and michaelmas daisies.

older: it is, however, an addiction, and has been for twenty years – she says she is on a 'high' from those first magical moments in spring when the first plants begin to show through from a flat bed of earth, right through to the final breathtaking display of old friends and new acquaintances in summer.

Four miles away, in Harrogate, a friend of Chris Abbot's, Margaret Bleasdale, has a more conventional mixed border, with a basic background and structure of shrubs, including *Viburnum tinus, Viburnum opulus, Aucuba japonica*, pink and white flowered lavateras, spireas and *Escallonia* 'Apple Blossom'. Between the shrubs, she has her herbaceous perennials, but she also puts in annuals, and tender plants which go in after the frosts – crocosmias and the magnificent *Lilium regale* are kept in compost in pots in the greenhouse from October to the beginning of June. There is a lovely winding path, of pulverized bark, wandering through the bed – it looks nice and it also enables her to get at plants easily. Margaret doesn't clear everything away at the end of the season – she likes to leave some plants which retain a striking structure through the winter, partly for their shape, often enhanced by frosts, partly to encourage wildlife.

The list of herbaceous perennials is long, and grows longer every year as new varieties appear – you should nose around other people's gardens, garden centres, and consult catalogues before you make up your mind what to go for. Height is important and although you generally want small plants at the front, larger ones at the back and so on, it doesn't do to get too regimented about it. What gardeners call 'dot plants' – those whose positioning breaks up the military organization, often happen by accident. Sometimes you will find that a plant doesn't perform by the book, or the seed packet, and surges up a foot or more higher than it should have been – if the effect is pleasing, then keep it where it is. Margaret Bleasdale found that she had an over-exuberant artemisia at the front of her border. At first, it irritated her and then she found that she liked it there – the scent as she brushed past it was wonderful, and would have been lost had the plant been in its authorized spot, further back in the border.

Colour is a matter of personal taste and again, you can pick up ideas from other people – some admire a riot of colour, others will carefully grade colours together, blues with whites or silvers, yellows and golds, 'hot spots' of reds and so on.

One of the delights of a herbaceous border is that you can cut flowers for the house. Margaret Bleasdale is a keen flower arranger

A combination of grey foliaged plants with the white flowered *Anaphalis margaritacea* in the foreground form a subtle border in Welwyn.

The Welsh poppy, *Meconopsis cambrica*, will seed itself all over your garden if you let it, and is perfect for cut flowers.

and likes to cut lots of flowers – she would decimate her border, so she grows extra plants for cutting in raised beds. She had some very good tips for people who like to grow flowers in the garden for transfer to the house: always pick in the early morning, so the plants are full of moisture and carry a bucket half-full of water to collect them in. Plants with hollow stems, such as lupins and delphiniums, should be held upside down after cutting and their stems filled with water – Margaret then plugs the ends with bits of kitchen roll. Plants with sappy stems, like euphorbias and poppies, should have the cut ends sealed – she does this by simply sticking them in the soil. Rose stems should be dipped in hot water for a minute. You can support the cut flowers in their container with florist's green foam, or with chicken mesh crumpled up in the vase. If you want to show off stems as well as flower, then put them in a clear glass container, with clear sellotape criss-crossed across the top. Margaret puts a few drops of bleach and a pinch of sugar in the water – the bleach keeps the water clear and the sugar feeds the plants.

Roses

I would think that almost every garden visited by *Garden Club* had a rose of some sort, somewhere – hardly surprising really, since it is unquestionably the nation's favourite flower. The statistics are staggering – in the 1990s, we are told, eight out of ten gardens have a rose, three and a half million roses are bought every single year. There are two thousand six hundred different named roses currently on the market. There are excellent roses to be had from the supermarket or garden centre, but if you are a bit more ambitious than that and want something a bit more unusual that you may have spotted in a magazine or on a television programme, then you need help. A very useful and inexpensive annual publication is *Find that Rose*, which is compiled by the Rose Growers' Association and is a guide to who grows what. Dr D. G. Hessayon's *The Rose Expert* is the clearest, best and cheapest introduction to the subject.

Part of the secret of the romance of the rose is that it is such a versatile and adaptable plant. *Garden Club* has come across it as a tiny pot plant, almost a bonsai rose, in an eight-centimetre pot on a kitchen window-sill, as a patio plant in a container or raised bed, as ground cover, as a bush, shrub or hedge, or as a climber or rambler. The largest of all, so far, was a rambler with the delightful name of 'Rambling Rector', which had hurled itself at least forty feet up a conifer and was smothered, in July, with fragrant small white flowers.

Pick your plant, and you can have one rose or another in flower for at least nine months of the year. Early roses can flower in March or April – try 'Canary Bird' or the pink-flowered *Rosa willmotiae*: late roses can give a vase full of heady cut blooms in November. One lady I met had photographs of her November vases going back years – her favourites seemed to be the white 'Pascale', 'Amber Queen', the bi-pink 'Silver Jubilee' and the salmon pink 'Fragrant Delight'.

There is tremendous argument about when and how you should prune bush roses and it is not a discussion I care to step into too deeply, especially since the Royal National Rose Society are experimenting at their garden in St Albans with a method of spring pruning which involves hacking them off with a chainsaw.

Here, courtesy of a lady in Cambridgeshire, is a programme which works for her and her 260 roses. Prune back to about one third of the shrub's height in late autumn, after flowering. The cut is the standard one, just above a bud, sloping away from the bud. In spring, cut away anything which is diseased or dying, and old shoots. Look at the top of the new shoots you have left – if there is a brown central core, you have die-back and should cut down to the next bud. You need to keep cutting back until you have got rid of die-back and the brown bit and are cutting into clean wood – this sometimes means that you can go almost back to the rootstock. All your pruning should be to outward facing buds, so that the plant is encouraged to grow in a goblet shape. Roses are greedy feeders and should be well fed and watered in spring, after pruning, and in summer, after dead-heading. Dead-heading, by the way is not just a matter of tidying up. If you do it regularly, cutting well back on the stem, you can persuade the rose to flower again . . . and again. One row of patio roses in this garden were flowering for the fourth time, in September.

Outside public parks and show-place gardens, the garden devoted entirely to roses is something of a rarity. There was, though, one more wonderful example in Leicestershire, where the owner had divided up a large garden into garden 'rooms', surrounded by hedges, and one of the rooms was devoted to roses. It is worth mentioning in passing, that those hedges had first been of Leyland cypress (*x Cupressocyparis leylandii*), which had proved simply too fast-growing, even for a keen and experienced gardener, and had been replaced by

hornbeam. Within the hedging walls, the rose garden was divided by a cruciform path of flags laid on gravel and the area so quartered was planted with species and old-fashioned shrub roses, underplanted with foxgloves, verbascums, campanulas and geraniums.

It is often argued, with some justification, that species and old roses are more trouble than the modern hybrid teas and floribundas (or large-flowered and cluster-flowered roses, as we are now encouraged to call them). They are more susceptible to pests and diseases, many of them are not repeat flowering, so only have a brief period of glory and they tend to be large and unwieldy creatures. But – and it is a very big but – once you have been exposed to their charms, all these arguments are swept aside and old roses become wholly addictive.

There are hundreds to choose from, each with its own character, beauty and history – the names alone are enough to whet the appetite. Among the Leicester gardener's favourites were *Rosa Mundi*, also known as *Rosa gallica* 'Versicolor', with a flower splashed with pink and white against a crimson background – this plant, which dates back to the twelfth century, was reputed to be the favourite flower of Fair

Old roses, foxgloves and verbascums mingle in a Leicester garden. The roses are 'Cerise bouquet' and 'Albertine'. The white flower on the left is *Achillea ptarmica* 'The Pearl'.

Rosamund, the mistress of Henry II; *R.* 'Madame Hardy', a scented Damask rose from the 1830s, with white incurved green-eyed flowers; *R.* 'Charles de Mills', with deep red and purple quartered blooms and a heady scent; two hybrid musks from the 1920s, 'Buff Beauty', with apricot and buff yellow flowers and 'Penelope', which has deep creamy pink flowers – both are repeat flowering; *R. fedtschenkoana*, with single white flowers over bluish-green foliage, the flowers followed by scarlet hips and *R. moyesii*, with blood red single roses, then flagon-shaped orange red hips.

It doesn't matter what sort of rose you favour, they will all need good, moisture retentive soil, well prepared with lots of well-rotted manure – the soil in this part of Leicestershire is sandy and not very good for roses, but the gardener was able to call in manure by the lorry-load from neighbouring farms when he was preparing the beds. On a visit to the famous garden created at Sissinghurst by Vita Sackville-West (something of a shrine for many *Garden Club* devotees), he noticed that many of the old roses were supported by hazel hoops. He copied the idea, but used steel hoops which he found in an old builder's yard – they rust, of course, but he finds the effect rather pleasing. He mulches well with manure in the early part of the year, feeds in spring and sprays, 'not as often as he should', he says, from when the foliage starts to unfurl, and dead-heads after flowering. The pruning of these roses, in early spring, is not as uniform as that of the modern varieties – some are hardly pruned at all, apart from dead or dying branches. Others, the ones which do flower twice in the season, are pruned moderately. He grows clematis, especially *Clematis viticella*, around and through many of the roses, so that in late August he has in effect a clematis garden, with a few of his roses which flower twice. There is an archway leading into the rose garden and over this he has grown a modern climber called 'Guinee', whose fragrant deep maroon flowers are intertwined with those of the clematis 'Perle d'Azur', which flowers, Mediterranean blue, at the same time.

A garden devoted to roses is unusual, but roses were often used as background shrubs in mixed borders. These being *Garden Club* borders, the roses, needless to say, were always interesting and often unusual. There is one rose – *R. omeiensis pteracantha.* – grown, not primarily for its foliage, flower or hips, but for its thorns, which are huge, vicious looking and red. On young shoots, they are translucent, and the sun shining through them is a sight to behold. *Rosa glauca*, also known as *rubrifolia*, is much loved by flower arrangers for its rich plum

Rosa 'Albertine' smothering a post and fence in an Oxford garden.

coloured shoots and foliage – the flowers are small, single and pink. The plant seeds freely and, being a species, comes true from seed, which means that although you have a lot of tidying up to do, you also have lots of plants to give away to friends. One of the most popular large shrubs, spotted in several gardens, was Rose 'Nevada', which has strong, arching branches and large bold cream flowers in early spring.

There is deep confusion among beginners about the difference between climbing and rambling roses. Many ramblers are viciously thorned and most flower only once a year, on last year's wood. They can be encouraged to sprawl, as ground cover, or to cover old buildings, or to climb old trees. In the best of all worlds, once a rambler is well established, you would prune back at least some of the old stems which have flowered, in autumn. This involves untying the whole thing, doing your pruning, then tying in the new growth, which can be a formidable operation. Many people I met contented themselves with shortening some of the lateral growth, then, after a year or so, when it was obvious that a gnarled old stem or two should come out, gritted their teeth and got on with the job. Some ramblers are so rampant that they have to be dealt with every year. 'François Juranville' is a wonderful rose with flowers which fade from deep pink, but it grows twenty feet a year – I saw one example, on a large pergola, whose owner said it was even more energetic than that. In June, you could almost see it growing – certainly you could measure its daily growth in late Spring by putting a pencil mark on the pergola and noting progress. 'Albertine' is another popular and extremely vigorous rambler, first introduced in the 1920s: it has pale pink, scented flowers.

Climbers can do most things that ramblers do, but also make good wall-covering plants, with proper support. Many of them are repeat-flowering, and they should be pruned in spring, removing any rebellious shoots which spoil their shape, and pruning last year's side shoots to two or three buds. Some of them are well behaved, and can be unpicked from a small trellis and cut back each year in autumn. 'Rosy Mantle' is a case in point.

Climbers and wall plants

Sooner or later, all gardeners get tired of looking at blank walls or fences – a rose trellis is one possible cloak or curtain, of course, but there are many others.

Some climbers, once well planted within range of a wall, can do the job on their own – ivies and the climbing hydrangea, *Hydrangea petiolaris*, have aerial roots which cling to tiny cracks and crevices, the Virginia creeper, *Parthenocissus quinquefolia*, has tiny adhesive pads which perform the same task. Others, which have twining stems, like honeysuckle and wisteria, or twining leaf stalks, like clematis, will need some help to get going and some guidance as to where to go. Wall plants, such as some forms of pyracantha, cotoneaster and ceanothus, are not natural climbers and will need training and support all the way.

Whatever form of support you put up on a wall – a wooden or plastic trellis, or horizontal wires pinned into the brickwork – make sure that it stands proud of the wall by three to five centimetres, so that there is a space behind the plant for air to circulate. I met one gardener, who would prefer to remain anonymous, who spent a deal of time and money pinning support wires flush to his wall, only to find that nothing he planted seemed to want to climb and those plants which did manage to get a few feet up the wall were always sickly and diseased. Another gardener provided a sheath of chicken wire mesh around a tree trunk to help a climber on its way – the tree grew, so that the wire became tight and actually began to cut into the bark, so that in the end, the climber couldn't climb and the host tree began to suffer as well.

Aspect is important – north- and east-facing walls or fences can be cold, and you need tough plants to do well, whereas the sun lovers will want the south facing spot. In Southampton, we saw a textbook example of how to do it. The lady here had taken a cutting from a passion flower, *Passiflora caerulea*, which had not been doing at all well for her as a houseplant, and put it outside, training it up a south facing fence, where it was obviously very happy. She also had kiwi fruit, *Actinidia chinensis* – a male and a female, which you need to get fruit. Elsewhere, on south-facing walls and fences, we saw *Wisteria sinensis* and *Fremontodendron californicum* (see Plant of the Week). Roy Lancaster recommended one of his favourite climbers for this favoured aspect – *Trachelospermum asiaticum*, an evergreen with glossy leaves and scented star shaped, jasmine-like summer flowers.

The north or east wall is the place for ivies, the climbing hydrangea, Virginia creeper, pyracanthas, cotoneasters and winter jasmine, *Jasminum nudiflorum*. Our Southampton gardener had planted a variegated ivy here – *Hedera algeriensis* 'Gloire de Marengo', and some tough clematis – *Clematis montana* 'Pink Perfection' and *Clematis* 'Hagley Hybrid'.

The best advice I heard about planting climbers came from a clematis lover in Grimsby, who said that 'you should spend as much on preparation as you did on the plant.' He dug a hole, two or three times as big as the rootball of the plant, a couple of feet away from the

A summer-flowering clematis – 'Rouge Cardinale'.

wall or tree that the new plant was going to climb. If possible, he liked to plant on the north, or shady side of the host plant, following the old adage that clematis like to have their roots in the shade and their heads in the sun. Plenty of well-rotted manure was dug in, and a handful of bonemeal scattered. The plant itself was soaked in a bucket of water for an hour before planting. You have to be especially careful not to break the delicate stem of the clematis at this stage, so he left the supporting cane in, sloping it from the hole to lean on the support plant at an angle of forty-five degrees. Sometimes the plant is tied on to its cane too tightly, so you loosen the ties a little to allow the plant to grow. The advice on initial preparation would hold good for almost any climber, although another gardener, this time in Norfolk, came up with a useful tip for ivy – he took away the support cane completely and laid the plant on the ground towards the wall, pinning it to the soil with an old-fashioned wooden clothes peg to stop the wind blowing it around. The ivy will find its way to the wall – and provide a weed-smothering ground cover on its way.

Clematis is our most popular climber and, certainly in the hands of *Garden Club* gardeners, a very versatile performer. I've already mentioned the popular combination of clematis and roses, but that is only half the story. The gardener in Grimsby grew clematis up through rhododendrons and up the trunks of old apple trees. He had a programme of colour to enhance the apple blossom and fruit, and the rhododendron flowers, from early spring through to late autumn – *Clematis macropetala*, with blue flowers, came out in early April in his garden, followed by two varieties of *C. alpina*, 'Francis Rivis' and 'Little Nell'. *Clematis tangutica* put out its yellow flowers in June – in autumn they provided a bonus in the shape of lovely silky seed heads. *Clematis × jackmanii* burst into those magnificent purple flowers in July and *C.* 'Gravetye Beauty' burned deep red in August. To complete the sequence, he had planted *C. cirrhosa balearica*, an evergreen, winter-flowering kind, so that it grew through a leylandii hedge. I've also seen clematis grown through heather, and as ground cover, with wire mesh keeping it just off the soil.

The species and their varieties, such as *C. montana*, *C. tangutica* and *C. macropetala*, don't need much in the way of pruning, apart from tidying up and the cutting out of overcrowded wood. The larger flowering hybrids divide into two groups – some, such as 'Hagley Hybrid' and 'Jackmanii' are cut back hard in February, leaving just a bud or two of the season's growth, others, such as the famous 'Nelly Moser', are trimmed back lightly after flowering.

The most rampant climber of all is the Russian vine, or mile-a-minute plant – *Fallopia baldchuanica*. You really can't go wrong with this one and it is often recommended for covering up unsightly sheds and the like. Its merits are many – explosive energy, lovely white, pinkish tinged panicles of flower in August and September, good autumn colour, no real care and maintenance. One word of warning though, from a gardener in Dorset, who had set it to climb a pergola – it does grow quite ferociously and he found that he had to keep cutting it back savagely, otherwise the walkway under the pergola got blocked up.

Other summer climbers seen on the programme present more of a challenge to get started. *Tropaeolum speciosum*, the Scots or Chilean Flame Flower, comes from Chile and seems to grow very well in Scotland. Most of us have to struggle to grow it annually from seed, but a gardener in Glasgow had been given some of the white, spaghetti-like roots by a friend and neighbour at the end of one winter. He covered them lightly with soil and they took well and produced a vigorous plant which twined its way around a blue spruce – a startling

*Tropaeolum
tuberosum* 'Ken
Aslet'.

combination of scarlet on powder blue. Now he simply cuts it down at
the end of the season and protects the roots with a mulch of peat.
Better known and not so pernickety is *Tropaeolum peregrinum*, the
Canary Creeper, yellow flowered, treated as an annual and grown
from seed. *Tropaeolum tuberosum*, is another South American climber,
with orange-red flowers – 'Ken Aslet' is a very popular variety, well
worth persevering with.

Eccremocarpus scaber, the Chilean Glory Vine, is grown from seed, is very vigorous and has lovely yellow orange flowers – it is a tender perennial and in mild areas the rootstock may survive the winter, given protection, although most people would have to treat it as an annual. Once it is established and happy, as it clearly was in the Southampton garden where we saw it, it self-seeds, so you can pot up the seedlings and keep them for the next year. *Cobaea scandens*, from Mexico, is another tender climber which most of us would have to grow from seed. It has extraordinary purple flowers with prominent green sepals and is known as the Cup and Saucer Vine. *Aconitum volubile*, the blue-flowered climbing monkshood, is also grown from seed and was spotted flourishing in gardens as far apart as Surbiton and Grimsby.

Some summer vegetables

When runner beans were first introduced into this country from South America, they were grown as ornamental climbers and people enjoyed the foliage and flowers, but were deeply suspicious of the long green pods – now they are the most popular of all our summer vegetables. Given that they come from exotic foreign parts, they are treated as half-hardy annuals, to be sown under cover and put out after the last frosts. Several *Garden Club* gardeners grew runner beans of staggering size and quality: what follows is an amalgam of their working practices.

Ground preparation is all important. The trench for the beans is dug during the winter; it should be at least a spit deep, and filled with organic matter, such as well-rotted manure or garden compost, mixed in with the soil. One gardener started this work early in October and used the trench itself as a long narrow compost heap, putting in kitchen waste, organic matter and the like so that it rotted down *in situ*. Another lined his trench with perforated polythene, which, he said, helped to conserve moisture.

If you live in an area with a long growing season, you can sow runner beans directly into the ground once conditions are favourable, but most people I met wouldn't take that risk. Their seeds were sown under glass in a soil-based compost at the end of February or the beginning of March. They took about three weeks to germinate, and were then kept protected until it was time to put them outdoors. Two or three weeks before they went out, a dressing of bonemeal and sulphate of potash was scattered over the trenches.

Everyone uses canes or poles measuring three metres or so, sunk sixty centimetres or more into the ground, but there are conflicting, almost religious, theories about the best method of support. Many people like the familiar tent-like framework – poles set firmly in the ground in pairs, sloping towards one another and crossing at the top, the crossings made more secure by horizontal poles lashed across the crossings. Others swear by the box-like structure, with the climbing poles vertically in the ground, with supporting horizontals half way up and at the top. Those with smaller gardens make do with a wigwam made from four poles, tied together at the top. In the last analysis, the sturdiness of the structure is probably more important than its shape. Once the poles are covered with foliage, the wind can pressure them like a sail and the whole thing can come crashing down.

Once the flowers appear, usually in early July, the plants are watered frequently. To help with pollination, some gardeners plant other bright flowers nearby – I've seen nasturtiums and both French and African marigolds lined up by runner beans. Some gardeners in Dorset noticed that one veteran countryman had grown sweet peas up the last two poles of a row and assumed that this was some bit of country magic – in fact, the man told me that they were there only because he had some sweet pea plants left over and he liked the colourful effect. Birds sometimes attack red-flowered runner beans – the answer to this would seem to be to plant white flowered varieties. When the flowers have set, liquid fertilizer is watered in once a week. The plants will eventually twine their way to the top of the poles – when this happens, their tops are pinched out. Any side shoots which develop are pinched out at once.

The rewards for all this care and attention can be spectacular. Some people have been known to harvest through August to the end of September, filling their freezer for the months ahead. One or two thrifty gardeners left half a dozen pods on the vine, choosing ones with strong bodies and short necks. The seeds ripen and harden and in late autumn can be gathered, prised from the pod and kept for sowing next year. Favoured varieties of runner beans seemed to be 'Scarlet Emperor', 'Streamline', 'Enorma' and 'Crusader'.

If you don't want to be bothered about the mechanics of poles and canes, climbing runner beans can be grown without much in the way of support as bush plants – you simply nip out the tips of the plants

Runner beans –
once grown simply
for their foliage
and flowers.

once the stems have appeared and keep the pods off the soil with twigs. Yields are, needless to say, much lower. 'Hammond Dwarf Scarlet' is a specially bred compact, self-stopping variety which doesn't need support.

French beans too, are treated as half-hardy annuals and are grown in much the same way as runner beans, some are climbers and some bush or dwarf forms.

The tomato is another South American native which was received with great caution when it arrived in Europe in the sixteenth century. Some people thought the fruit was an aphrodisiac, others considered it poisonous – these hopes and fears eventually dissipated and now people grow it and eat it without qualms.

Growing tomatoes is a tricky business – even trickier if you decide to do it outdoors. A gardener from Surbiton, in Surrey, showed how it can be done, adding a couple of tips of his own. Seed was sown, under glass, in an appropriate compost. As the plants grew, they were transferred, first to nine-centimetre pots, then into thirteen-centimetre pots. They were hardened off in a cold frame, then put into bottomless pots, bedded into growing bags in a sunny position by a shed. They were staked, each plant being loosely tied to a about a metre and a quarter long cane. The bottomless pots were only half full at first – as the plants grew up in the canes, more compost was added and the plants grew what are called adventitious roots – in effect, extra roots further up the stem. Watering and liquid feeding was done via smaller pots, sunk into the growing bags between the bottomless pots and thus acting like funnels. This seemed to solve the eternal problems of over- or under-watering which tomatoes so often suffer from. As usual, the side shoots which appear at the joints of the leaves were pinched out. When five trusses had set, the tops of the plants were stopped by being pinched out. (Incidentally, the further north from Surbiton you go, you might stop such outdoor plants at four or even three trusses).

If all your outdoor tomatoes ripen, then you are very skilled or we have had an exceptional summer – by September, you will usually find that you have a proportion of green unripened fruits. Do not despair, for they can be ripened by bringing them indoors, wrapping each fruit in tissue and putting them in a drawer with a ripe banana.

Herbs

As far as herbs are concerned, most of us, I suspect, would be content to grow just a few – parsley, sage, rosemary and thyme. When Daphne Whiteacre moved into her house in Huntingdon, many years ago, she found that she had a back garden of thin, sandy soil and couldn't afford the shrubs and perennials she wanted, so she started with herbs, largely because they were cheap and easy to grow on poor soil. Many herbs are of Mediterranean origin and are used to scratching a living from poor conditions – as long as they get plenty of sunshine.

Today, Daphne has a collection, at the last count, of a hundred and three different herbs, all set out charmingly between winding gravel paths in a garden of their own, at the bottom of a conventional garden of shrubs, trees, flowers and a lawn. Every single herb has its use – some for the kitchen, some as curatives or health and beauty preparations and others for the garden itself. Above all, Daphne's herb garden is a garden in its own right. It is a pleasant place to sit, especially in summer, to watch the flowers, the bees and the butterflies and a fascinating place to work, throughout the year, with sowing, planting, cultivation, harvesting and propagation to think about.

Some gardening lore first – Daphne plants santolina and southernwood (*Artemisia abrotanum*) underneath her roses and reckons that their pungent aroma helps to ward off aphids and blackfly. Everyone who grows broad beans knows what pests black aphids are – you see them clustered at the top of the plant and unless you do something the beans are done for. It is conventional gardening practice to nip the tops out of the plants, which discourages the black beasts, and encourages the beans to set. Daphne plants French marigolds under her beans, and they deter the aphids. She grows comfrey, one of those wonderful, luxuriantly foliaged cut-and-come-again plants. The leaves are used on the compost heap, but from time to time she dumps a cargo of leaves into a bucket of water to make a liquid feed for the rest of the garden. You abandon the bucket of water and leaves in an inconspicuous place in the garden for three or four weeks – the smell is terrible – and then the stuff is ready.

Parsley is the best known of the kitchen herbs, but a lot of people have trouble germinating the seed. The seed *does* take a long time to germinate and country folk used to say that it went 'seven times to the devil and back' before it sprouted. The main trouble, Daphne reckons, is that people sow the seed when the ground is still too cold in the spring and they tend to sow the seed too deeply. You could try the old remedy, of pouring a kettleful of hot water over the seeds when they are in the ground, or you could do what she does, which is to sow in August or September, when the soil has had a whole season to warm up, then protect the crop with a cloche through the worst of the winter.

If it still doesn't germinate, drastic measures are necessary – let your wife (or husband) sow it. Another bit of country lore says that 'whoever wears the trousers' in the household will be successful with parsley. If you let part of the crop grow on into a second year, then it will flower and seed – Daphne collects her own seed and sows it in early autumn.

Rosemary grows as a perennial shrub, but it may well need protection in the winter. Daphne always takes cuttings in autumn, just to be on the safe side – she also does this when the original plant gets too woody. She has developed her own unorthodox but obviously effective cuttings compost – four parts peat, one part coir, one part vermiculite, plus a teaspoon of Phostrogen, mixed in a bucket. It is all very simple – pinch off five-centimetre growing shoots, strip off all the leaves bar a few at the top, and put the cuttings in a tray of compost in the greenhouse, or on a window-sill.

Daphne doesn't like using rosemary straight from the shrub for cooking, because she thinks that the leaves become hard and sharp in the oven. She dries small branches by simply hanging them up in the kitchen, then, working with her hands and the dried plant in a clear polythene bag, strips off the leaves. They are then ground up in a coffee grinder, and the resultant flakes used in the kitchen.

Sage is another perennial, treated in much the same way as rosemary in the garden. Preparation for the kitchen is much simpler – you rub the dried leaves through a sieve. Daphne grows purple sage too. Brew a few leaves in a jugful of hot water for six minutes and you have a palliative for a sore throat – gargle with the mixture, then swallow.

Daphne also makes pot-pourris. The recipe changes from year to year, according to mood and what there is to harvest, but a typical list of ingredients would include petals from roses, jasmine, philadelphus, larkspur, delphiniums and leaves from angelica and rosemary,

together with dried, ground-up orange peel. They are all laid in one of those flat wooden tomato boxes, with its bottom slats removed and replaced with a piece of an old lace curtain, stapled on to the wood. Box plus contents are put in the airing cupboard and the petals and foliage dry without losing too much of their colour. (Daphne does not approve of drying in the microwave – she says this cooks the ingredients, rather than dries them). The mixture is then put in a wooden bowl, with shop-bought powdered orris root as a fixative – and there you have the scents of summer on call, whenever and wherever you want them in the house.

Purple sage (*Salvia officinalis* 'Purpurascens') – useful for sore throats.

Autumn

Signs

There comes that time in late summer when you go out into the garden early in the morning and realize that you should have put on a sweater or even a coat – there is a dampness, a sudden unwelcome chill in the air, which means that autumn has arrived. There are other signs as well – the first leaves start to turn colour.

One of the very earliest autumn indicators is one of the Japanese cherries, *Prunus sargentii* – when its leaves start to burn red, you know that summer is coming to an end. In Harrogate, in 1992, that aptly named tree *Liquidambar styraciflua*, the American Sweet Gum, showed outer leaves that looked as if molten amber had been poured on them from above and a crab apple, *Malus* 'John Downie' was displaying its red fruits. The following week, in Dorset, a Virginia creeper was already in full scarlet display and autumn crocuses were flowering. Nothing unusual in all this – except that it was still August.

By common consent among most gardeners, the weather in August 1992 was unusual – colder, wetter and windier and with less than average sunshine. A gardener in Dorset, who takes daily rainfall readings for the Met Office, reported that there were only six rain-free days during the month and 30 August was the wettest day of the whole year. The season seemed to be two or three weeks further on than it actually was. Having said that, gardeners on the East coast reported that it had been dryer and warmer than usual.

All of which goes to show that you must garden by your instincts and local knowledge and conditions, and not by the book. Another point – it may have been a miserable summer for holiday-makers, but many gardeners pointed out that the rain, at least, was just what they wanted – many trees and shrubs which had been stressed and suffering over the last few seasons from lack of moisture were now putting on extraordinary growth and looked healthier than they had for years. Some were forecasting great things from *next* year's bulbs and shrubs, which were building up as a result of this year's rainfall.

Muck and magic

Mention the word 'compost' to almost any *Garden Club* gardener and you immediately become involved in a long and enthusiastic discussion about this most fascinating of topics.

Grass cuttings and leaves, given the right treatment, will rot down into compost. One *Garden Club* member, whose garden is quite small, waits until the leaves are quite thickly strewn on the lawn, then mows and bags up the mixture of cut grass and chopped-up leaves. He ties up the polythene sacks, perforates them, then hides them away in an inconspicuous part of the garden until spring, by which time the mix has rotted down enough for the material to be used as a mulch around shrubs. Not too much grass, he warns, otherwise it remains a soggy green mass.

Autumn leaves on their own can be used to make leaf mould – wander around any woodland area and you will see this happening quite naturally, as the leaves fall and gently rot away after a year or so, into the earth whence they came. All you need to speed the process up a little is some sort of enclosure to coral the leaves and stop them blowing around – an open topped wire mesh cage will do the job nicely. All you have to do is pile in the leaves and wait. After a year, the material should have rotted enough to use as a mulch; after two, you should have material fine enough to use instead of peat, as potting compost.

We saw a tried and tested orthodox compost heap in the making in the programme from Cornwall. There were three bays side by side, open at the front and on top, each about 120 centimetres square, made with stout wooden posts and slatted wooden sides – you could just as easily make them with chicken wire round the posts. The base was wooden planks upon bricks. The important point about this is that air must be able to circulate freely underneath and around the compost. With three bays instead of one, the Cornish gardener was able to keep a production line of compost going – one was being made, another was half way there and the third was the finished article.

Much of the material was standard organic waste from the garden and kitchen – grass cuttings, leaves (not thick-stalked ones like sycamore and horse chestnut), vegetable debris such as rhubarb leaves and potato haulm, vegetable peelings (but not thick stalks from cabbage and cauliflower) and tea-leaves (some of them in the form of teabags). There were some unusual ingredients – seaweed, for one, and feathers from a couple of discarded pillows. Almost anything that is organic and will rot down can be included, although you should avoid diseased material, pernicious and perennial weeds or seedy stuff in a heap like this one.

All the ingredients were thoroughly mixed as they were added to the heap – when the pile had been allowed to subside and was about twenty-five centimetres high, a thickish layer of manure mixed with straw was added as an activator – an activator simply being something which bacteria can get to work on quickly and gather energy for the tougher stuff – you can buy proprietary activators. A piece of old carpet was placed on top of the heap as each bit was completed, to keep the rain off. Once a bay was full, it was left for a month or two, then the material was forked out and turned over. A well-made compost heap will heat up considerably – you can tell if you've been successful because you can feel the warmth and on coldish days, actually see steam coming off it.

There are commercial compost bins available; a lady in Suffolk swore by a Rotol compost maker, which looks a bit like a Dalek out of the *Doctor Who* television series – a black cone of corrugated plastic, with a lid and a door at the front. She kept chickens, in a movable coop with a wire mesh bottom – she put the coop on a different part of the lawn each week and she claimed that the chickens kept the lawn weeds down. Their droppings, together with grass cuttings and waste matter from the vegetable garden and the kitchen, went into the compost maker and eventually rotted down. She had three bins on the go.

If you can afford it, then the best present for a keen gardener these days is a shredding machine. There are several on the market, ranging from small electric ones to larger petrol driven monsters. The case for such a machine was put most powerfully by a gardener from Aberdeen – you can put all the usual material through the shredder, but now add tougher stuff as well, including those tough vegetable stalks, hedge trimmings and woody material and even seedy material that you might think twice about putting on an orthodox compost heap. He had a biggish garden and used to have to take the trimmings to the tip, making perhaps four or five trips – then he would go to the garden centre and come back with a bale or two of peat. Now, everything goes into the shredder and he uses what comes out, when it has rotted down, instead of peat; he doesn't have peat beds for acid-loving

Cool colour arranging offsets the Twibells' artemisia collection. *Nicotiana sylvestris*, golden sage, white valerian and *Lavatera trimestris* 'Mont Blanc' form a backing to 'Powis Castle' in the foreground.

species, the artemisia, can be a hardy or a half-hardy annual, a biennial; some are considered garden plants, others weeds and they range in size from a prostrate ground-hugging plant to a monster three or four metres high.

The National Collections and the NCCPG

John's collection has been designated the National Collection of artemisias, one of almost six hundred such collections of species, sub-species and cultivars of plants set up under the auspices of a comparatively new but already hugely effective organization called the National Council for the Conservation of Plants and Gardens – the NCCPG. Some of these collections are in show-place gardens such as the RHS's Wisley garden – they hold the National Collections of hostas, snowdrops, heathers and pulmonarias, among others. Some are attached to horticultural teaching establishments, botanic gardens, arboretums or commercial nurseries, while some are in private gardens. The purpose of all these collections is to preserve as complete a living record as possible of plants, for horticultural, taxonomic, historical and scientific purposes.

The NCCPG publishes an inexpensive Directory of all the National Collections, which tells you who holds what, where – and how you can get in touch and visit. There are sections at the back which list the Collections by county, and tell you which are the best months to call in and see the plants when they are in flower. It is a map – and a timetable – to a treasure trove of information.

The National Collections are only part of the web of activities of the NCCPG – they publish a twice-yearly Journal, organize an annual Garden Heritage Week and co-ordinate the activities of over forty local groups, scattered all over Great Britain. These groups organize lectures, visits, workshops and plant and seed exchanges for their members. Time and time again, I came across *Garden Club* gardeners who were also enthusiastic members of the NCCPG – some of them, like John Twibell, hold National Collections.

The central organization of the NCCPG is at Wisley – you can write to them, for details of membership and the list of local groups, at The Pines, c/o Wisley Garden, Woking, Surrey GU23 6QB.

Herbaceous borders – the final show

Anne Stevens and her husband Alan escaped from London almost thirty years ago and bought a thatched cottage on an acre and a half of land in the quiet Dorset hamlet of Ansty, near Dorchester. Ivy Cottage is idylically beautiful and the garden is splendid and full of interest all through the year. (Anne, by the way, has the National Collection of *Trollius*, or Globe Flower.) *Garden Club* visited her in autumn, when there are two huge herbaceous borders in magnificent bloom. One of them is an island bed, rather than a conventional border backing on to a hedge or fence, which means than you can walk right round it and admire the plants. Here, the larger plants are in the middle of the bed and the others are graded roughly by size to the tiny ones on the edges – an interesting variation on the usual theme and an idea particularly espoused by Alan Bloom, the world-famous plantsman who owns Bressingham Gardens, in Norfolk.

Anne Stevens holds the National Collection of Trollius in her garden.

Anne and Alan
Stevens' cottage in
Dorset – the
garden can be
viewed most
Thursdays from
spring through to
autumn.

If you are after ideas for autumn flowering herbaceous perennials, then this is the place to explore – the garden, by the way, is open to the public most Thursdays and she gets visitors not just from all over Britain, but from Europe and America.

There are old autumn favourites, like asters, Japanese anemones and sedums. Some asters suffer from mildew or wilt, but Anne recommends *Aster sedifolius* (*acris*), *Aster × frikartii* and *Aster ericoides* 'White Heather' as being particularly reliable – 'White Heather' flowers in her garden in November! Japanese anemones (technically called *Anemone × hybrida*) are lovely, but sometimes invasive – particularly beautiful ones here included the deep pink 'Bressingham Glow', 'Queen Charlotte', which is also pink, and 'White Queen'.

This being very much a plantswoman's garden, there were some unusual plants within the display, including *Physostegia virginiana*, the 'obedient plant', which is so called because its flowers bend over obediently when pushed to one side – and right themselves quietly later on. 'Vivid' is a deep pink flowered version of this strange creature, 'Summer Spire' is a deep violet. *Tricyrtis formosana* has strange

Japanese anemones and asters are favourites for a traditional cottage garden border.

**The toad lily
(*Tricyrtis
formosana*) can be
grown from seed.**

orchid-like flowers, with huge stamens – some petals pure coloured, some curiously speckled, hence the common name, the Toad Lily. You can grow the Toad Lily from seed and it should take eighteen months to first flowering. Two unlikely parents, that old favourite the golden rod, or solidago, and the aster produced the strange × *Solidaster luteus*, a perennial with dusty yellow flowers. Right in the middle of the island bed was the Ginger Lily, *Hedychium gardnerianum*, a huge thing with bold lanceolate leaves and spiky yellow flowers. Many visitors were baffled by this – some thought that it was a banana tree. It was sunk in a pot within the border, and is taken indoors when the frosts come. The cardoon, *Cynara cardunculus*, a near neighbour in the bed and almost as big, resembles a globe artichoke – it is cut down each year, but surges back up.

A little further up the same lane in the same hamlet, Arthur Thomas lives in another lovely cottage which belonged to his father and his grandfather before him. The front garden is pretty enough, with roses, geraniums and begonias and a Boston Ivy, turning colour now as autumn began smothering the front of the house. At the back,

The ginger lily
(*Hedychium
gardnerianum*),
sunk in a pot in
Anne Stevens'
herbaceous border,
brought indoors
when the frosts
come.

Arthur Thomas's cottage and front garden, in Dorset, just up the lane from Anne Stevens.

Mr Thomas has the nearest thing to a *real* cottage garden the series has seen – an orchard full of gnarled old fruit trees with roses and clematis swarming up them and a large triangular patch full of flowers and vegetables all mixed up together. Along the base of this triangle, there is a rampant herbaceous border with groups of phlox, crocosmia, delphiniums, heliopsis, allium, inula, astilbe and the like growing lustily in glorious profusion. Elsewhere, among the vegetables, he has his architectural plants, including a huge dock, with a tall spire of brown seedheads – he called it the 'Mutton Dock' and said that was its name in Dorset. It may have been the Great Water Dock, *Rumex hydropathum*. Whichever one it was, it had been put there deliberately as it reminded him of his farming days. There was also an enormous globe artichoke, with blue thistle-like flowers atop the stems. Although it was in the vegetable garden, Mr Thomas grew it as an ornamental plant – he said, with a twinkle in his eye, that people had told him that you made a special sauce to eat it with, then threw away the head and ate the sauce. All of which goes to show that you can experiment with all sorts of things in a herbaceous border, if you have the courage.

In late autumn, when the display has finished, Mr Thomas cuts everything down and mulches the whole bed with well-rotted compost and manure, taking care to mulch round the plants and not in amongst them. Being a retired farmer, he has access to unlimited supplies of manure and he has his own somewhat unorthodox compost heap – he loads all the herbaceous material he has cut down into a trailer and dumps it in a pile in a small field he still owns. There are various heaps, of various vintages from past year, in the field, so he looks for one that is well rotted down and trails it back to the border.

When the autumn display is over, most of us have to take a careful look at our herbaceous and mixed borders and decide how all the plants can best be helped through the winter – some will be cut down, mulched and divided, if necessary, in spring. Tender plants are a different matter: some *Garden Club* gardeners, as we have seen, leave them where they are, but give them some form of protection. Others take out a double form of insurance, by bringing the plants into a frost-free place, treating them as stock plants, taking cuttings in autumn or spring.

Arthur Thomas's herbaceous border – glorious confusion.

Dahlias

**Arthur Thomas's
dahlia tubers are
left in the ground
through the winter.**

The perennial dahlia is a favourite border flower which comes in a wholly bewildering array of shapes, sizes and colours. The National Dahlia Society lists them into no less than ten groups – single flowered, anemone-flowered, decorative, ball, pom-pom, cactus, among others. The showing of dahlias is an absorbing and time con-suming hobby and the finer details can only be learned from fellow enthusiasts. Even if you only grow them in the garden for your own pleasure, however, you have a decision to make in late autumn: to lift or not to lift the tubers? Mr Thomas has dahlias in his herbaceous border and he treats them like everything else – they are cut down low when the frosts have blackened them, well mulched and left where they are. They seem to thrive on it, and some gardeners might take encouragement from that.

Elsewhere though, people take more trouble, and lift the tubers in late autumn. This can be quite a difficult operation, for dahlia tubers can grow to a formidable size and tubers and adhering soil can be very heavy. You prise off as much of the soil as you can, using a stick or a pencil to probe some of the more inaccessible parts, then store the tubers upside down in a dry place for a couple of weeks. After that, the rest of the soil should come off without too much trouble and you can cut off all the stringy roots to leave a compact tuber – some people bore a hole through the tuber, from where the stem originally emerged, right through to the base. This helps to drain moisture and stop rot setting in. The tubers are then treated with a fungicide, and set out on a bed of dry peat, sawdust or ash in a wooden, open-topped box – old tomato boxes are ideal. Some people store them in open-topped envelopes made out of old newspaper. Storage conditions through the winter are important – you need a dry, frost-proof place, such as a cold greenhouse, a garage or a shed. The following year, you set them off into growth again in early spring by filling the trays with moistened peat and taking cuttings or dividing the tubers.

Chrysanthemums

M any people would argue that the chrysanthemum is *the* autumn flower. There are tough old hardy perennials for the herbaceous border, such as the Shasta daisies (*Chrysanthemum maximum*), moon daisies (*C. serotinum*) and *Chrysanthemum coccineum*, which we used to know as the pyrethrum, and there are hardy and half-hardy annuals, like the corn marigold (*C. segetum*), the summer-flowering *C. coronarium* and *C. carinatum*, but the most fascinating groups of all are gathered together under the general name of florist's chrysanthemums, which are grown as cut flowers for the house if you are a casual gardener and for exhibition and competition if you are serious.

They in turn are grouped into early-flowering types, usually grown in the garden for early autumn flowering, and late-flowering kinds, which end up in the greenhouse for late autumn flowering. If you are growing florist's chrysanthemums purely for your own pleasure in the garden, then you would stick to the early-flowering types – the small flowered varieties are easiest to cope with.

There are sub-divisions according to flower size and further categorizations into flower type – Large exhibition, Incurved, Reflexing, Singles, Pom-Poms, Sprays and so on. It is all quite bewildering for the

Chrysanthemums packed for transport to the National Chrysanthemum Society show in London.

beginner and the advice given time and time again by chrysanthemum growers was that the only way to learn about these fascinating plants is to find an exhibition grower, or local society near you and learn from others. Albert Bird, a retired miner and champion grower from Neath, was given some plants by a friend at the pit, went along to the local society, which met in a pub in Neath, and this began a lifetime's interest, which has taken him all over Great Britain for shows and competitions. Chris Wiles, in Dorset, wandered into a chrysanthemum show in Yeovil for want of anything better to do one wet Sunday only eight years ago and came out dazzled by the perfection of the plants on show – three years later he was a National Champion. All chrysanthemum enthusiasts say that the local societies (and the national society) are friendly and encouraging to newcomers and have members from all walks of life.

Albert Bird
checking on the
progress of his
chrysanthemums in
spring, in his
garden near Neath,
South Wales.

Chrysanthemums
on display and in
competition at the
Royal Horticultural
Society hall in
November.

Last minute
checking of blooms
at the National
show by a member
of the Neath
Chrysanthemum
Society.

You could pick up the basics from a reference book – dig up the chrysanthemum stools after flowering, dry them off, store them in boxes of peat or compost in a cold frame, bring them into comparative warmth early in the year, take cuttings, pot the cuttings on, support and feed them, take out side shoots and disbud and so on – but you will only learn timing and the real tricks of the trade from other people. To see people like Albert Bird and Chris Wiles preparing their blooms for show was an education in itself. The cut flowers are kept in deep water for forty-eight hours, then each head is gone over with scrupulous care with a cotton-wool bud. Petals are dusted, picked and preened until they are as near perfection as human hand and eye can shape them. Mind you, there is perhaps hope for us lesser mortals – Chris and his wife Julie have encouraged their children to grow and show early chrysanths and if a four- and a six-year-old can do it, then so can we.

Bulbs up: bulbs down

There can be a great deal of digging in the autumn, and not just in the vegetable garden. There are the dahlia tubers and chrysanthemum stools to prise up and store. The corms of gladioli should certainly come out, be dried off for a couple of weeks, then cleaned and stored in a cool, frost-free place and, if you live in colder areas, you may want to play safe and bring in the bulbs of some types of crocosmia and agapanthus. On the other hand, now is the time to plant new narcissi and other spring flowering bulbs – narcissi can go in during September, tulips are planted later, usually in November, although you will recall that there is some dispute among *Garden Club* gardeners about whether one can leave established tulips in the ground all year. If you like the look of the colchicums, or autumn crocuses you see in other people's gardens (or on *Garden Club*) at this time of year, then buy the bulbs now and plant them – you could well get a display within a month. Hyacinths too, can go in again now.

Fuchsias

There are many ways of tucking up fuchsias for the Winter – it all depends, firstly on the hardiness of the variety and secondly, where you live. Anne Stevens has a large shrub of the species, *Fuchsia magellanica*, at the back of one of her herbaceous borders, which she leaves as it is – in a bad winter it may be cut back by frost, but then the dead wood is pruned away in spring and it thrives as ever. Julie Wiles grows lots of *Fuchsia* 'Lena', a lovely hybrid with nodding purple and white flowers which last well on into autumn, in a circular bed around a flowering cherry. After the fuchsias have finished flowering, she simply cuts them back to the ground and gives them some protection, with bracken or straw, and up they come the following year, with a little encouragement in the form of a handful of bonemeal and generous watering.

The bedding varieties and the ones displayed in pots as part of a summer display can be looked after in several ways. First, you should taper off the feeding and watering, then, as the flowers fade, snip them off with a pair of scissors. Later, as the leaves turn yellow, strip them off by hand until you are left with what looks like a small dead

Opposite: The stag's horn sumach (*Rhus typhina*) – sensational in autumn, but watch out for those suckers.

tree. It may look ruthless, but the dead and dying leaves may harbour pests and diseases and they must be got rid of completely. As you deflower and defoliate, you can shape the framework of the plant at the same time, cutting just above points where shoots break.

The plants can now be stored, on their sides in their pots, in any cool, dry and frost-free place – a loft, garage, or underneath the greenhouse staging. If you don't have the space, you can simply cover them with peat or bury them in the garden. An elderly lady in South-port had a special patch for this purpose, just by the side of her greenhouse – she said if she put them somewhere else in the garden, she might forget where they were he following spring.

To breathe life back into your fuchsias next year, you spray them gently with tepid water and after a couple of weeks, the plants will start to shoot again and you can sculpt and shape them as they grow, pinching out the tops to make them bushy.

Autumn colour

At Westonbirt Arboretum, in Gloucestershire, they are used to people ringing up anxiously, from September onwards, to ask what is going to be the best week for autumn colour, for within this huge collection of trees and shrubs there is a magnetic attraction at this time of year – the Japanese acer glade. The peak of autumn colour here – a pyrotechnic display of yellows, gold, oranges, reds and coppery browns – is usually in the third week in October, but each year is different and of course the display depends upon the preceding seasons.

The glade is spacious, grassy and fringed by Japanese maples, in turn protected by larger native trees beyond. The acers do best in partial or dappled shade and prefer to be sheltered from cold or drying winds. There is much to admire, and many people come away especially impressed by *Acer japonicum* 'Vitifolium', the Vine-leaved Downy Maple, whose foliage passes through the whole autumn spectrum of colour, from yellow in September, through to patches of crimson, orange and deep ruby red in October. *Acer palmatum*, of which there are many here, is a variable species – some turn red, others yellow. They are smaller trees than the 'Vitifolium', and more suitable for the smaller garden. The *Plant Finder* lists over a hundred and fifty cultivars from the species, many of them with interesting-

Autumn at
Westonbirt
Arboretum, in
Gloucestershire.
Japanese acers
burning bright.

sounding Japanese names. Among the most popular with *Garden Club* members are *Acer palmatum* 'Dissectum', which has frothy, lace-like green leaves and 'Atropurpureum' which has copper-coloured leaves – there is another one, which combines the merits of the first two, called 'Dissectum Atropurpureum'. If you can get to Westonbirt, you can explore a living reference book of Japanese acers – they hold the National Collection here, which includes over a hundred and fifty cultivars. It is always as well, though, to check back home with local gardeners, if you can, to make sure there are no unforeseen problems before you rush out and buy.

Rhus typhina, the Stag's Horn Sumach, is a magnificent shrubby tree, with glorious autumn colour and most unusual cones of red fruits. A Swansea gardener loved his Sumach, but was driven to distraction by the vigorous suckers it put up each year. They came up everywhere, sometimes yards from the tree itself, cracking pavements and poking up through the grass on his otherwise immaculate lawn. In Huntingdon, a gardener had bought a spindle bush, *Euonymous europaeus*, having seen a specimen in a local park. The one in the park, performing according to the book, had good autumn colour, with lovely fruits – scarlet capsules opening to reveal orange berries. His plant didn't seem to want to fruit at all and he had only discovered later that this is a common fault with many of the spindles – you need two or three together for pollination to ensure fruit setting, because some of them have flowers which appear to be sterile. This is not the same problem as the berryless holly, which turns out to be a male plant, but the end result is the same. A gardener in Southport had planted a tupelo tree, *Nyssa sylvatica*, on the strength of one look at a similar tree in full autumn glory in another garden: once he had his own tree, he decided that, apart from the brief burst of autumn colour, it was one of the most boring trees he had ever seen, and it could eventually grow to ten metres or more and would then cast a shadow over his vegetable patch – the tree came out and he has kept quiet about the episode ever since.

It was clear from talking to many *Garden Club* gardeners that they are a canny lot and if they want something for autumn colour they also want value for money at other times of the year. *Acer griseum*, the Paperbark Maple, was a popular choice, seen in several gardens. Not only does it have red and yellow autumn tints, but when the leaves are gone there is the added bonus of the flaking, cinnamon-coloured bark which looks ravishing in winter sunlight.

Stuartia pseudocamellia has white flowers with yellow anthers in late spring, glorious autumn colour and, a bit like the *Acer griseum*, attractive, flaking bark to admire in the winter.

The Smoke Bush, *Cotinus coggygria*, has greyish flowers wreathed like wisps of smoke, on striking foliage which turns into an autumn fire of yellow and red. It is also one of those shrubs with trailing lower branches which lends itself to propagation by the method known as layering – you bend the branch down, scrape off some of the under-side bark and peg the branch down into the earth, covering it with a mix of compost and sharp sand. In eighteen months or so, the branch should have put down roots of its own – you sever it from the parent plant and there you have another one for the garden or to give to friends.

Hamamelis mollis, the Chinese Witch Hazel, produces tassels of fragrant yellow flowers on bare wood to cheer the most miserable February day and that is why you see it in so many good gardens, but it also has large, deeply veined leaves which unfurl through the late spring and summer and turn to a soft buttery yellow in autumn. A rose grower in Leicester pointed out that the species *Rosa virginiana* has single pink flowers in late summer and beautiful red, yellow and crimson leaves in autumn, and small red hips. The berberis, many pyracanthas and cotoneasters have good autumn colour, with their rich clusters of bright berries – and you have the bonus of spring flowers as well.

Smaller conifers

Once the autumn leaves have fallen and been cleared away for next year's compost or leaf mould, you are suddenly grateful, as the gloom descends, for evergreens and conifers. Dwarf, or slow-growing conifers are especially popular, since they can be combined with other plants, such as alpines or heathers, or included in mixed borders.

Bernard Cooper, in Grimsby, used to concentrate on chrys-anthemums and tomatoes. One year he went on holiday for a fort-night, leaving his son-in-law in charge of watering – the young man forgot about it, then, the day before his father-in-law's return, rushed in and swamped the greenhouse. Everything was ruined, so Mr Cooper scrapped the lot and decided to go for dwarf conifers outside in the garden instead, reckoning that they, at least, would come to no harm if he went away for the odd week. That was twenty-six years ago and now he has over a hundred different kinds growing in quite a small back garden. Each has its own character, growth habit, foliage form and seasonal variation and it all adds up to a quite fascinating miniature landscape. There are conifers growing as single specimens in small blocks of tufa, conifers in alpine troughs and in a small alpine and scree garden, and conifers among other plants in a border.

The word 'dwarf' requires some explanation. Mr Cooper divides his plants up further – 'pygmy' conifers are those which grow no higher than twenty-three centimetres, 'dwarfs' are taller than pygmies but will only get to one metre high, while 'slow-growing' conifers range from one to four metres. The problem is that many garden centres and nurseries call them *all* dwarfs, which can lead to confusion – you really need to know how large a plant is going to be if it is fit into your plan of campaign. To be absolutely sure, you need advice from a specialist nursery, or another gardener. Perhaps a brief list of some of Mr Cooper's favourite plants will help you on your way.

Of the pygmy conifers, he likes *Chamaecyparis obtusa* 'Minima', which grows like a tiny mossy green pincushion or hedgehog. He has his own version of this, an equally small but slightly more open plant, developed from a sport on the original and called *C. obtusa* 'Cooper's Gem'. The dwarfs he is particularly fond of are both pines – *Pinus leucodermis* 'Schmidtii', another mound plant, a tiny explosion of green, with the new growth paler than the old, and *Pinus mugo* 'Mops', another compact green globe. In his front garden, he has two slow-growing conifers – a yew, *Taxus baccata* 'Standishii', an upright, columnar tree, with green and gold foliage, which should grow no more than six feet tall and a juniper, *Juniperus chinensis* 'Aurea', which is a six-foot mix of green and gold foliage and has pale creamy flowers in spring – this one will need support until it is about three years old.

On the other side of town, in the countryside not far from the Humber estuary, Frank Osgerby has over two hundred different dwarf and slow-growing conifers flourishing within a more conventional setting, many of them mixed in with other plants. Frank likes to work to a ten-year plan with his garden, so is in a position to offer a progress report on some of the conifers he particularly enjoys. *Juniperus squamata* 'Blue Star', easily available almost anywhere in the country, has reached just forty-five centimetres in ten years – it is densely foliaged, blue and bun shaped. *Thuja orientalis* 'Aurea Nana' is a bright yellow ball of whorled foliage, about eighty centimetres across. *Chamaecyparis thyoides* 'Rubicon' is forty-five centimetres tall and has wonderful foliage – the old shoots are red, the new ones green and the whole plant takes on an intense purple hue in winter. *Chamaecyparis lawsoniana* 'Treasure' is an eighty-centimetre column of sulphur yellow, with green tints, and remains absolutely unperturbed by either hot sun or cold winds.

I've listed a handful of the plants from the two Grimsby gardens in some details to illustrate that conifers do differ tremendously one from another, and to give the lie to that scurrilous rumour put about in some gardening circles that they are 'boring'. If anything, I would say that dwarf conifers are the boom plants at the moment, judging by the numbers I saw, not just in Grimsby, but throughout the country.

Finally, one of Roy Lancaster's special favourites, the Korean Fir, *Abies koreana*, must be mentioned. It is compact, cone shaped and has lush foliage, green on top and silver underneath, but the real surprise comes with the cones, which are thickly encrusted on the upper branches and are a most lovely shade of blue. In Harrogate, Roy came across a tree which was eight years old but still only waist high – it should eventually get to three to five metres, which means that it would fit into quite a small garden.

Heathers and heaths

David and Rita Plumridge moved to their present home, 250 metres up and on the edge of open moorland, near Consett, in County Durham, some ten years ago, and found conventional gardening something of a struggle. The last frosts of spring can be as late as May or even June here and the first autumnal frosts have been known in late September – the growing season for bedding and herbaceous plants can be as short as three months. The answer is to concentrate on plants which thrive in difficult conditions – hence their decision to grow heathers and heaths.

Our native heathers and heaths tough it out on poor soils in exposed conditions on moorland and mountainside and although there are very few species, nurserymen have bred hundreds of varieties from them, so that the spectrum of colour from flower and foliage is huge, while habit and flowering times vary. The Plumridges have a collection of over a hundred different heathers, interplanted with slow-growing conifers, which together produce a magnificent,

ever-changing show of colour throughout the year – a triumph over
adversity and a display which is stunning through the autumn and
winter months. And to cap it all, a display such as this, once it is
established, needs little in the way of care and maintenance, because
the heathers eventually become efficient ground cover and smother
the weeds. All you need do is make sure they don't dry out in the
summer, and prune back last year's flowering shoots the following
spring.

As for the selection of plants, the difficulty is knowing where to
begin – the Plumridges' initial inspiration came from a single plant of
Calluna vulgaris, the native heather, which they brought with them
from Scotland. There are over four hundred named varieties of this
single species, each of them different in colour and form, listed in the
Plant Finder. To begin with, you might like to consider some of the
Plumridges' favourites: 'Silver Knight', an upright plant with
lavender-like flowers and grey foliage; 'White Lawn', a prostrate,
slow-growing plant; 'Sirson', whose foliage turns from brown to brilliant orange in autumn; and 'Anthony Davies', which has white flowers
on silvery-grey foliage. Then there are the bell heathers (*Erica cinera*):
try 'Purple Beauty', with its deep rose-purple flowers; 'Golden Drop',
which has golden foliage which turns rusty red as the weather gets
colder; or 'Domino', with its white flowers and ebony coloured caly-
ces. The Connemara Heath (*Daboecia cantabrica*) has many forms too –
'Bicolor', which sometimes has white, rose-purple and striped flowers
on the same plant and 'Alba', with brilliant white flowers, come highly
recommended.

All the plants listed so far need acid soil to do well, but, contrary
to popular belief, there are members of the heather family which are
tolerant of alkaline soils – all the varieties of *Erica carnea* and *Erica ×
darleyensis*, for example. All heathers and heaths are propagated very
easily from cuttings taken in autumn, or by layering, so if you are
patient, you can buy just a few plants to begin with, and then gradually build up your stock.

Opposite:
**Matthew, Rebecca
and Roy want you
to admire these
winter-flowering
heathers.**

Vegetables and the hunger gap

Drying onions for the local show.

Down at the Tinpot Lane Allotments, in Blandford Forum, Dorset, Cyril Hovard grows chrysanthemums and sweet peas for showing, together with vegetables for the kitchen – with good management, he can come up with vegetables all through the year. The chalky soil is improved each year with lots of spent mushroom compost, cow manure, blood, fish and bone, and compost which he makes himself in bins constructed from old wooden pallets. Whenever he has room to spare, he grows a green manure crop and digs it in. Overwintering vegetables are protected by cloches which he makes himself from panes of glass rescued from an old greenhouse – which he built himself fifty years ago. It is an impressive operation.

    The home freezer has been a tremendous boon for the vegetable gardener – by mid autumn, Mr Hovard has runner beans, French beans, sweet corn, calabrese, cauliflower and sugar snap peas safely harvested and frozen. Potatoes are harvested when they are ready, washed and dried and kept in sacks in a frost-free shed – he grows the French salad potatoes, 'Ratté' and 'Charlotte', the pink 'Desirée' and 'Condor' and the large white 'Kerstein'. There aren't many carrots and those he has will be left in the ground until Christmas, although other people on the allotment lift and store them in the usual way, putting them in boxes or bins of sawdust or dry peat. He will be sowing broad beans in November and is looking forward to harvesting early Brussels sprouts ('Roodnerf'), late Brussels ('Predora'), purple sprouting broccoli, 'Walcheren' winter cauliflower, Sanger's early winter cauliflower (a locally flourishing variety that doesn't do too well away from the south-west), parsnips and leeks – and all that lot should see him and his wife through the winter and well on into the New Year.

In spite of that formidable list and Mr Hovard's great skills and long experience as a gardener, he had problems in 1992 – his summer cauliflowers were attacked by caterpillars and since he doesn't like to use sprays, he picks them off by hand. It was one of those years when there were too many of them to pick. Above all though, he frets from time to time about what he calls his 'hunger gap', through May and early June, when vegetable pickings can be slim. This time, with the encouragement of the *Garden Club* team, he is going to try something new – oriental greens.

Joy Larkcom is a gardener who has researched, grown and written about oriental vegetables extensively: she has also edited the latest edition of the amateur vegetable grower's favourite bedside reading, the Royal Horticultural Society's publication, *The Vegetable Garden Displayed*, and has included there for the first time a section on oriental greens. That is the place to look if you are interested in growing a range of these most fascinating vegetables. There are Chinese cabbages, which can be heart-shaped, cylindrical, or fluffy topped, Chinese broccolis and lots of other as yet mysterious leafy plants which gardeners are now getting to grips with.

For growers who share Mr Hovard's problem of the May gap, there are several possibilities – he is experimenting with Komatsuna (spinach mustard), mizuna greens and mustard greens, especially the delightfully named 'Green-in-the-Snow'.

The first two can be grown in much the same way – seed sown under cover in early spring, transplanted outside and harvested fairly quickly. They are 'cut-and-come-again plants', so you can keep on harvesting the leaves – they should give four or five cuts before they run to seed. You can use young leaves in salads, or let them grow larger and cook them – stir fry, steam or boil, according to your fancy. Komatsuna tastes like European cabbage with a hint of spinach, while the feathery leaves of the Mizuna greens have a mild mustardy flavour.

The mustard greens, including 'Green-in-the-Snow', grow more slowly and are not therefore suitable for the cut-and-come-again treatment. The leaves can be very spicy and peppery, so they are mostly cooked rather than put in salads. They are all brassicas and can be attacked by the usual pests – slugs, caterpillars, cutworms and cabbage rootfly – so it is as well to protect them with fine netting, or one of those fleecy films, hooped and secured over the bed.

Tools of the trade

Most, although not all, the gardeners you see on *Garden Club* have been pursuing their hobby for a long time, and have gradually built up their own set of favourite garden tools – they have many hints and tips for beginners on this most important subject. What follows is not an encyclopaedic run-down on all those tools which are available from the garden centres, but some ideas which may help the beginner chose from what is on offer. Above all, you must feel comfortable with your spade, fork, secateurs or whatever and it is a good idea to work with temporarily borrowed tools to find out what works best for you, rather than rush out and buy expensive items which may not live up to their publicity.

Spades come with handles shaped like a D or a T: on the whole, people seemed to think that the D handles were easier on the hand. The top edge of the blade – where your foot will press a million times – is too sharp on many spades and you can end up with a painful bruise on your instep or the ball of your foot after a hard morning's digging. Try to find a spade with a foot-tread along the top. Stainless steel spades are very expensive, but everyone I met who used one was convinced it was the best investment they had ever made. The blade seems to cut more easily into the soil and they don't need much in the way of maintenance – just a quick wipe with a damp cloth. The same holds good, of course for all stainless steel tools.

If you have back trouble, digging can be difficult and painful. One or two people used what are sometimes known as Irish, or West

Arthur Thomas's
toolshed, in Dorset.
His seed packets
are kept in netting
on the ceiling.

Country, spades – the ones with almost heart-shaped blades and very long handle-less shafts. You can get leverage on the handle without having to bend your back as much as you would on a conventional spade. There are also attachments which you can buy for ordinary spades and forks which will help: an extra handle which fixes on to the front of the shaft, and a curled spring which goes on the back of the blade and flicks over the soil once you have plunged the spade in.

The standard size sturdy four-tine fork is useful for digging or turning over heavy or stony soils, but if your soils are fairly easy, or you are simply dealing with borders, you may be much better off with a smaller version, sometimes called a ladies', or a border fork. Potato growers may add another weapon to their armoury – a flat-tined fork which you push through the soil to bring up the spuds without spearing them.

Garden trowels have a distressing habit of curling up at the tip of the blade after a lot of use – once that happens no amount of metal bashing seems to put them right and you can't dig cleanly into the ground with them. The answer, again, is to buy a stainless steel one if you can afford it. (A trowel has a curved blade, of course, but many people don't realize that this is a deliberate piece of design – when you are digging out the hole for the bulb or whatever, slide the blade into the earth vertically and use the curve, as you dig, to complete a circle, which you can then excavate easily. A gardener in Shrewsbury showed me this blindingly simple but almost forgotten technique.) Another gardener, this time in Cambridgeshire, sharpened the side of the blade of his trowel, and serrated the edge with a file, thus providing himself with a tool with which he could dig *and* chop off weeds.

There are all sorts of different shaped hoes: draw hoes, which are sometimes called swan-necked hoes, and are used for weed control or drawing seed drills, and push hoes, sometimes called Dutch hoes. But the most useful of the lot for cutting off weeds is the push-pull hoe, a wonderful invention with a flat blade, sharpened fore and aft. Use it in the mornings – cut off the weeds and let the sun kill off the cuttings, then put them on the compost heap. You can, after all, draw out your seed drills with the corner of an ordinary garden rake.

Beginners agonize over the respective merits of different kinds of secateurs – some cut with a blade against an anvil, others have a shearing, or scissor-type action. There is really nothing much to choose between them and the important point to consider is how long they will last and how easy they are to sharpen. Once secateurs get

blunt – and cheap ones get blunt very quickly – they tear, rather than cut and that can damage plants. Almost all the professionals use distinctive red-handled secateurs made by a Swiss firm called Felco – take a close look next time you see someone pruning or dead-heading on television. They are very expensive but very good and the sort of thing you should perhaps ask for as a Christmas, birthday or retirement present. You can also buy what are called cut and hold secateurs – as you cut the roses, the implement holds the cutting in its jaws, which means that you can do the job one-handed.

Arthur Thomas using a swan-neck hoe among his vegetables.

Making do

You might have thought that there is nothing much to the art of putting canes into the ground – bash them with a mallet and that is that. What happens is that the top and sometimes the bottom, of the cane flattens or splits, so you have to throw it away and buy a new one for the next season. I've seen some gardeners slot an empty shot gun cartridge on top of the cane, which means that the brass base of the cartridge, rather than the tip of the cane, takes the force of the mallet. One gardener in Cambridgeshire had actually fettled up a tool of his own to solve the problem. It was basically a pointed metal rod, with a T-shaped handle and a footrest about fifty centimetres or so above the point. You held the handle, pushed on the footrest and pressed out a fifty-centimetre hole for the cane to go in to.

When you are preparing pots or trays for sowing seed, or planting seedlings, you should make sure that the compost in the containers is gently firmed flat. What you need is a wooden presser, with a simple handle on top and a flat surface underneath, which will fit easily into the top of the circular pot or the rectangular seed tray. Make them yourself, from bits of scrap wood – you don't need a degree in woodwork. Several *Garden Club* gardeners had gone one better than that, and made themselves rectangular pressers, with thirty or so short wooden pegs spaced regularly on the underside, so that they could firm the compost in the tray and make holes for seedlings at the same time. Dibbers, the little gadgets you use for making single holes for seedlings, were whittled out of shrub prunings. I saw other people using old pencils, three-inch nails, or the hulls of abandoned biros.

Sooner or later, everyone gets round to the fascinating and rewarding business of propagating plants by taking cuttings and rooting them. For perfect results, you need a perspex covered propagator, with some form of under-soil heating, but before you graduate to that stage of sophistication, you can do very well without such an expensive piece of equipment.

At least one gardener I know has had startling success with spring or summer cuttings from shrubs by simply nipping off short, non-flowering shoots, two or three inches long, stripping off all but the top couple of leaves and sticking the cuttings in the ground under the mother plant – he doesn't even bother dipping the stems of the cuttings in hormone rooting powder. Some fuchsia and chrysanthemum growers do this too – popping cuttings around the mother plant in its pot.

A stage further on from that is the sort of mini-greenhouse for the cuttings, made by putting a clear polythene bag over the cuttings in their plantpot – you should put a framework of four small sticks in the pot, to ensure that the leaves of the cuttings do not touch the polythene. When you take a careful look at the packaging you get around goods from the supermarket, you realize that there are many things

A plastic lemonade bottle recycled as a miniature greenhouse.

you can recycle as temporary propagators – egg boxes with cardboard cups and clear polythene tops, meat trays with clear polythene lids, those large litre or two litre plastic bottles.

One gardener had the bottle propagator down to a fine art: he cut a door in side of the bottle, so that he could put a little compost in the bottom. On top of the compost he posted through the door an eight-centimetre plant pot complete with cuttings in moistened compost. He wrote an abbreviated form of the name of the plants, and the date of planting, on the top of the plastic stopper. His miniature propagator stood on the kitchen window-sill and when the sun shone in, he turned the bottle so that the old label, which was still attached, became a form of greenhouse shading. Cut the bottom off one of those big bottles, by the way, and you have a ready-made cloche for protecting a single plant outdoors. All this isn't absolute recycling by the way, because after you have used whatever it is, courtesy of the supermarket, for propagation, you should throw away the container, otherwise diseases are likely to build up.

Another recycling trick with supermarket materials – hardwood cuttings, in the usual cuttings compost of half and half peat and sharp sand, were protected out in the open by cardboard boxes, sunk in the ground. As the season progressed and the cuttings rooted, the cardboard gradually disintegrated – in effect composting itself as it sheltered the cuttings.

Further Education

During the whole course of the *Garden Club* travels, no one had called upon the services of a garden designer – everyone had worked out, gradually, through trial and error, what sort of garden they wanted, what they could afford, and what would work in their local conditions – and most said they were still not satisfied and were thinking their way forward to something better. That is the nature and the joy of this sort of gardening.

Equally, no one gardened in isolation, but relied very much on other people and other places for help and inspiration. There is, as Sue Shephard felt when she first commissioned *Garden Club*, an extraordinary comradeship and constant interchange of information among gardeners – everyone is interested in what happens over other people's garden walls. You can satisfy your curiosity, as we have seen, by joining a local gardening society, or the local branches of the national societies, such as the Hardy Plant Society, the Alpine Garden Club, the NCCPG and many others.

You can also visit great gardens, such as Wisley, Westonbirt Arboretum, or the gardens of the National Trust and find small detail amongst the grandeur which will help you along your way.

You should certainly buy the annual guide to the National Gardens Scheme – the *Yellow Book*. The NGS started life in 1927, when

some six hundred rather grand gardens, including King George the Fifth's private garden at Sandringham, opened their gates to visitors at a shilling a head, to help raise money for the Queen Alexandra Memorial Fund which was set up to aid the cause of district nursing. Nowadays, the National Gardens Scheme is still going strong and the money raised is split between various charities supported by the Scheme and other good causes helped on by the gardeners themselves. Today, sixty years or so on from its beginnings, the list of gardeners has been augmented by hundreds of small gardens, all open, for a small fee, for two or three days a year and sometimes more.

A considerable number of the gardeners featured in *Garden Club* are participating members of the National Gardens Scheme, which means that on certain selected days, you can see the results of their efforts for yourself, and perhaps even get the chance to chat to the gardeners. On Open Days, many of them sell modestly priced plants they have propagated from within their gardens, to raise a bit more money for their chosen charities. They are an extremely knowledgeable and friendly bunch of people, very generous with their time.

Jean Rawlinson's garden near Southport is one of many included in the National Gardens Scheme.

Plant of the Week

The Plant of the Week has been a permanent and popular feature of the *Garden Club* programmes since they first began in spring 1991. Week in, week out, Roy Lancaster enthuses, as only he can, about a plant which he feels is appropriate to the time of year, rewarding, interesting, sometimes amusing, and well worth a place in your garden.

The first two years of *Garden Club* ran from spring through to autumn, with an extended break, rather like school holidays, in the weeks of high summer. I have included plants spotlighted in the programmes and bridged the summer gap, with Roy's help and advice, to provide a collection of thirty-two plants, at four a month, from March to October.

All of them are available somewhere. Many of them will be on sale at your local garden centre, others will require tracking down. Once you get involved in the wholly delightful pastime of plant hunting for your garden, you will need help. Beg, borrow, steal, or better still, buy a current edition of an absolutely wonderful reference book called *The Plant Finder*, devised and compiled by Chris Philip and edited by Tony Lord and published by the Moorlands Publishing Company in association with the Hardy Plant Society.

This book, an awesome work of reference, first appeared in 1987 and rapidly became the gardeners' bible. The latest edition costs £10.99, lists over 55,000 plants, from alpines to trees and once you have cracked the somewhat complicated code of nursery indentification, tells you precisely where you can buy them. I would stress that you need an up-to-date edition, because nurseries come and go, and so do plants.

MARCH: WEEK I

Sarcococca confusa

For most of the year, you might wonder if *Sarcococca confusa* is worthy of its place in your garden. It is a small evergreen shrub, with privet-sized, pointed leaves, darkish glossy green on top, a lighter lime green underneath. You can use it as ground cover, or even let it grow up to be a modest hedge: it is tolerant of most soils and does well in shade.

It has a secret: in the depths of winter and up to early spring, it produces white flowers, half-hidden among the leaves, which have a truly wonderful scent – some people say of vanilla, others honey and there are those who compare it to Eastern perfumes.

Sarcococca comes from the Greek, and means fleshy berries. The black berries appear from April to July and the chances are you will not even notice them, because by that time there are other things to distract your eye in the garden.

The second part of the name – 'confusa' – means, as you might expect, 'confused'. This might refer to the fact that it can easily be confused with other Sarcococcas, of which there are several. *S. humilis*, which comes from China, is a dwarf version of the species and has white flowers with pink anthers: *S. ruscifolia var. chinensis* has dark red berries: *S. hookeriana var. digyna* 'Purple Stem', as its name suggests, has attractive dark purple stems, with narrow, willow-like leaves. They, and others like them, all tend to be called Christmas Box, or Sweet Box, by the time they get into British gardens.

MARCH: WEEK 2

Viburnum tinus 'Eve Price'

Roy Lancaster chose *Viburnum tinus* 'Eve Price' as his plant of the week for an early spring programme from Penzance and planted it on a high hillside overlooking the sea, where it would certainly be subject to salt sea breezes and even gales – not the most promising of locations, you might have thought. In fact, 'Eve Price' seems to be one of those plants which will do well almost anywhere, in sun or shade and in most soils. Remarkable really, when you think that the Laurustinus (*Viburnum tinus*), from which it is derived, came originally from the Mediterranean.

'Eve Price' is evergreen, with dark green glossy leaves. The flowers, carried in dense terminal clustered heads, are pink in bud, opening white, and span the winter, sometimes lasting from autumn right through to early spring. After a good summer, the flowers are followed by steel-blue berries, which gradually turn black. There is some debate as to whether the flowers are scented – Roy Lancaster is a recent convert to the pro-scent lobby.

It is a more compact and densely leaved shrub than the Laurustinus, growing to about 2 to 2.5 metres high and about 1.2–2 m across. You can use it in the garden as a single specimen, or buy several plants and grow them as an informal hedge, putting the young plants in at about 60 cm apart.

'Eve Price' was named, in 1961, after the wife of the late Sir Harry Price, who at one time owned Wakehurst Place, the famous garden in Sussex which now belongs to the Royal Botanic Gardens, Kew.

MARCH: WEEK 3

Ilex aquifolium 'Ferox Argentea'

Propelled by tradition, we all go out and buy holly to decorate the house at Christmas. The one we buy is invariably *Ilex aquifolium* – it tends to be called English Holly, but in fact is native over a huge swathe of Europe. Holly is a versatile, though often slow-growing, plant and can be grown as a single specimen plant, a tree, or a hedge.

Ilex aquifolium 'Ferox Argentea' is a male plant, so it won't provide you with berries, but it will help to pollinate female plants. Its leaves, on dark purple twigs, are dark green, with creamy, rather than silver edges: they are strangely contorted, and have pale cream

hostile spines erupting all over them, hence the popular name for the plant, the Silver Hedgehog Holly. Not something you would want to bump into on a dark night.

When you pick the females for your 'Ferox Argentea', bear in mind that there is a huge choice, especially if you go to a specialist nursery. 'J. C. van Tol', which was bred in Holland at the end of the nineteenth century, is known for producing an abundance of fruit: 'Camelliifolia' has large dark glossy green leaves, few-spined or spineless. 'Handsworth New Silver' has white edging to the leaves, while 'Madame Briot' has gold margins. All those should give you the traditional red berries. There are also hollies with orange berries: 'Amber', which emerged from Hillier's Nursery in 1955, is one of them. 'Bacciflava', which used to be known as 'Fructolutea', has startling yellow berries.

MARCH: WEEK 4

Dryopteris erythrosora

Roy Lancaster has chosen a member of the fern family from the other side of. the world – *Dryopteris erythrosora* is found in the wild in mountain woodlands in China, Japan and South-east Asia. It is evergreen – fern fanciers tend to use the term 'wintergreen', but it means the same thing. The new, young fronds, which appear in spring, are coppery-pink, eventually turning deep green. The plant is reasonably hardy and given a sheltered, shady, position outdoors, will get to 60 cm high. Although it is really a woodland plant, I once saw an example cared for as a pot plant in a cold greenhouse, up in the wilds of the North-east, and it looked sensational.

The best time to plant outdoors would be spring or autumn. Dig the soil well and incorporate grit if the soil is heavy, and a dressing of rough peat, bark fibre or leaf mould. Water the new plant in well. After that, all you need to do is to keep the weeds away for a couple of years with a spring and autumn mulch, incorporating a dusting of bonemeal with the Spring mulch.

APRIL: WEEK I

Erysimum 'Bowles' Mauve'

Edward Augustus Bowles (1865–1954) was a largely self-taught horticultural genius, who created an extraordinary garden at his home at Myddleton House, Enfield, wrote and illustrated some gardening books which became classics and knew and was known by everyone in the horticultural world of his time. No one has the faintest idea why this plant is apparently named after him – it is not mentioned in any of his writings and friends of his who are still alive say it was never in his garden. A mystery yet to be solved, then.

People commonly refer to the erysimums as perennial wallflowers – this particular one is an evergreen sub-shrub, with long narrow greyish-green leaves, which flowers pinkish-purple and profusely in early spring – there may be odd, sparse, flowerings right through the year. By taking heeled cuttings in summer, it is possible to increase it to a small hedge. Roy Lancaster says that you should take cuttings anyway, because it can get cut down by frosts and in any case it tends to flicker out after a few years.

There is some mystery too, as to the plant's origins – it may be a hybrid of species from Spain, the Canary Islands, or South-west Europe. It is certainly one of those plants that will not thank you for kindness – it does best in a sunny, well-drained spot, with poor soil and little in the way of nourishment, which suggests that it must come from somewhere hot, dry and dusty.

APRIL: WEEK 2

Microbiota decussata

This prostrate, spreading, dwarf conifer was offered as Plant of the Week on a bitterly cold, wet and windy spring day in North Wales. As it turned out, that was really rather appropriate weather, for the plant was first discovered, in 1921, growing high on a mountain, above the tree line, in Siberia, not far from Vladivostock – since it survives there, one can be fairly sure that it will withstand whatever the British climate can throw at it.

Microbiota decussata has very interesting foliage – 'decussata' means that the scale-like leaves are in pairs, one pair at right angles to the next. As the plant develops, the foliage becomes densely packed and lace-like. In summer it is bright green and in winter can turn bronze, although if it is planted in a shady spot it will stay green all year.

If it is ground cover you are after, then this is the plant for you – a specimen at the famous Trompenburg Arboretum, in Holland, grew no more than 20 cm high in ten years, but during that time it spread to 3.5 metres across.

Roy Lancaster has one in his garden at home: planted in acid, sandy soil in the winter of 1984/85, it grew to 148 cm across in five years. Roy has grouped together a Mexican dwarf pine, several winter-flowering heaths and the dwarf rhododendron, R. yakushimanum, in the same bed and is pleased with the combination of colour and form, although, judging from the enthusiasm of the Trompenburg plant, the conifer could eventually engulf the whole display.

APRIL: WEEK 3

Osmanthus delavayi

Osmanthus delavayi is an evergreen shrub, which produces an explosion of delicately scented tiny white flowers in mid spring.

Most examples you see in British gardens are fairly small, but it can reach 3 metres and under certain conditions, a lot more than that. I saw one which had been given as a tiny shrub as a wedding present to a couple in Edinburgh. They had planted it in a sheltered corner by their house. By the time their Silver Wedding came round, the shrub had grown so that its top was well above their bedroom window – it must have been at least 6 metres high.

Osmanthus delavayi is not too fussy about soil and will do well in sun or half-shade. The Scottish couple I spoke of earlier said they used to keep their plant well watered during the summer, so that it did not dry out. A north or an east wind in winter can damage the foliage and leave some branches looking stark and bare, so it is best to offer some protection.

The name 'delavayi' commemorates one of the unsung heroes of plant collecting, a French missionary and botanist called Jean Marie Delavay, who worked in China in the late nineteenth century and first collected the plant which now bears his name from a wooded mountainside near Dali, in Yunnan Province, in 1890. Delavay, it is said, sent back hundreds of thousands of plants to Paris during his long stay in China – many of them were lost, due to lethargy, lack of interest and sheer incompetence by officials in Paris. The plant is well known in the Western world because George Forrest, another famous plant-hunter high on the list of Roy Lancaster's heroes, rediscovered it and sent back seed to Britain in the 1920s.

APRIL: WEEK 4

Chiastophyllum oppositifolium 'Jim's Pride'

Chiastophyllum oppositifolium is not a name that rolls easily off the tongue, nor is it particularly well known in gardening circles. Originally, the plant came from the Caucasus: it is a low-growing succulent evergreen, which produces little yellow catkins of flowers hanging from graceful stalks, in June.

Roy Lancaster first came across it when he was a young apprentice in Bolton's Parks. Up there in the north, it was grown in rock or stone walls in shady places, although it can also be put into troughs or containers, or used as ground cover.

About five years ago, in a private garden in Hampshire, an ordinary example of the plant produced a quite extraordinary sport, a spontaneous mutation from the original, with cream edging on the green leaves. The head gardener who made the discovery was called Jim Collins – the plant was subsequently developed and marketed under the wholly appropriate name of 'Jim's Pride'.

The example of 'Jim's Pride' which Roy Lancaster showed was being grown in a container, within a collection of dwarf conifers, also in containers, kept on the north side of a house. In the autumn, the lady gardener there was going to propagate the plant by division – taking the plant out of its pot, and splitting off rooted pieces from the original. Eventually, she hoped to have enough new plants to form ground cover on a shady spot around the side of the house.

Arisarum proboscideum

Arisarum proboscideum is a very odd little plant, with a bright glossy green arrow shaped leaves and chocolate coloured flowers, or rather spathes, which narrow at the top to a tail like a piece of brown string – it looks its best in late May. It likes moist, fertile soil, enriched with leafmould.

It is a plant which needs to be positioned where it can be seen – in a Southport garden, one was grown just at the point where a path turned a corner. Other people grow them in pots, so they can pick them up and show then to curious visitors.

It is the common name which makes them such a talking point – proboscideum means having a trunk or snout, but someone, somewhere, came up with the wonderful name of the 'mouse-tail plant'. Once you are told that, you immediately see that the brown flowers look just like mice diving into holes. Children love them, once they are told the tale, and become very anxious to introduce new people to this strange creature.

The mouse-tail plant comes originally from southern Italy, but seems to have settled well in Britain – it is hardy, and easy to grow.

Photinia × fraseri 'Red Robin'

Photinias offer an unexpected bonus – the blazing red foliage you might expect as autumn colour arrives in spring.

The one you tend to see in larger, older gardens is *Photinia davidiana*, better known as *Stranvaesia davidiana*, an evergreen which offers brightly coloured spring foliage, clusters of white flowers, followed by red berries and good autumn and winter colour. It does tend to get large and straggly, but is still a good plant if you have space to cope with it – you can expect it to reach between 5 and 6 metres in height.

For the smaller garden, there are several hybrids, or crosses between *Photinia serratifolia* and *P. glabra*. The first of these to appear was *Photinia × fraseri* 'Birmingham', which was introduced into commerce by the Fraser Nurseries of Birmingham, Alabama, USA, in the 1950s, and is available here from specialist nurseries. In America, by the way, it is known as 'Red Tip'. In Britain, there are two well-known hybrids from the same cross – one from Australia, the other from New Zealand. The Oz one is called 'Robusta' and the Kiwi, which is Roy Lancaster's favourite, is 'Red Robin'. So there you have it – a plant with Chinese and Japanese parents, hybridized first in America, improved upon in Australia and New Zealand – and available in British garden centres. A quite remarkable story.

All these hybrids can cope with a wide range of soils, as long as they are well drained and don't get waterlogged. They will get to 2 to 3 metres tall, but remain reasonably compact.

MAY: WEEK 3

Abutilon × suntense

Abutilon vitifolium, sometimes referred to confusingly as the Grape Leaved Flowering Maple, is not a maple at all, but a member of the mallow family: a free-flowering deciduous shrub with saucer-shaped pale violet flowers, it has been known in this country since 1836, when it was introduced from its native home of Chile. It needs cossetting, is usually grown in a sunny sheltered spot and does better in the milder areas of Britain.

In the late 1950s, another member of the family, *Abutilon ochsenii*, appeared here, sent to this country from Chile – it had smaller flowers, of violet blue, with yellow stamens.

Peter Dummer, the Master propagator at Hillier's, crossed the two in 1967, producing a hardier hybrid which was called 'Jermyns', after Sir Harold Hillier's house. The cross occurred accidentally in other places, including the late Geoffrey Gorer's garden at Sunte House, in Sussex. These new plants were given the botanical name *Abutilon × suntense*, by C. D. Brickell, then the director of the RHS garden at Wisley, now the Director-General of the RHS, and a world-renowned taxonomist. Thus you will find in the catalogues *Abutilon × suntense* 'Jermyns'. 'Sunte House', 'Gorer's White', 'Violetta' and 'White Charm' – selections, as some of the names suggest, with different coloured flowers, some white, some different shades of violet.

The new plants are hardier than the old, and should do well further north, as long as they are given a sheltered spot. They flower from as early as April until July and do well in poor soil, and could get up to 3 metres or more. They do not live a long time – perhaps less than ten years, so you should propagate by means of cuttings taken after flowering. The plants seed readily – 'like mustard and cress' says Roy Lancaster. If you nurse your chance seedlings on, you never know quite what you might get – perhaps a new selection you could give your own name to!

MAY: WEEK 4

Rhododendron yakushimanum

First and foremost, *Rhododendron yakushimanum* has exquisitely beautiful flowers – they appear as blush-pink buds, then gradually unfold into the purest white. In late May or early June, the whole shrub can be smothered in quite dazzling blossom.

After the flowers have gone, there is still so much to admire. The mature leaves are a rich glossy green and you will often see yakushimanum lovers turning over the leaves to see and touch the underside of the leaf, which has a soft brown covering like brown suede or felt, called the indumentum or tomentum. New leaves erupt all over the plant after flowering and they have a top covering of silvery brown – a striking contrast to the compact green dome below.

R. yakushimanum was one of the last major rhododendron species to be discovered. It was found in the wild on a Japanese island called Yakushima and introduced into this country in 1934, via the world-famous Exbury Gardens, near Southampton. Waterers Nursery, introduced it into commerce and now it is generally available, although you may have to find a specialist nursery rather than your local garden centre to get hold of one.

It is an easily manageable plant, rarely growing more than 1 metre high, but always remaining compact, so it will fit nicely into the scheme of things in a small garden, or even thrive in a tub or container on the patio. Like all rhododendrons, it is a lime-hater, so is best planted in a cool, moist-place, in acid soil, and mulched with peat, leaf-mould, or well rotted manure. Many people don't

realize that you should dead-head rhododendrons after they have flowered, just as you do daffodils and for the same reasons.

In the 1950s, Percy Wiseman, who was the nursery manager at Waterers, bred many hybrids by crossing the yakushimanum species with other compact hybrids – one of them is named after him and has lovely flowers, this time creamy pink in bud, turning to creamy white. There are many other notable hybrids, which tend to be referred to in the trade as 'Yaks', an inelegant term for a pretty breed. Best known are the seven dwarfs – 'Bashful', 'Grumpy', 'Dopey', 'Doc' and the rest. With some of the hybrids, the indumentum has been lost along the way.

JUNE: WEEK I

Cornus 'Porlock'

There is a member of the dogwood family, called *Cornus kousa* (and its variation *C. kousa var. chinensis*), which will make a smallish tree, rather than a shrub, if you prune it. It is invariably pictured, in all its June magnificence, in the gardening books and quite right too, for it is breathtaking – smothered in what appear to be creamy white stars of flowers which stain pink as they get older. In fact, the 'flowers' are bracts and the real blooms are almost insignificant green buttons in the centre of the bracts. Later, the flowers give way to strawberry-like fruits which look good enough to eat.

In the 1960s, a *Cornus kousa* and a similar, but less hardy dogwood, *Cornus capitata*, pro-
duced chance seedlings in the garden of Norman Hadden, near Porlock, in Somerset. One of the seedlings was presented to Hillier's Arboretum, where it was given the name 'Porlock': the original cross was called 'Norman Hadden'. It would take a trained botanist to tell the difference.

Roy Lancaster was given a *Cornus* 'Porlock' by a lady in Devon and it now grows about 6 metres high and in his words 'out-performs even *Cornus kousa*', with bold white bracts in June and glistening red fruits in autumn. It prefers a neutral to lime-free soil and a position in sun or half-shade and could be treated as a specimen tree in a large lawn, or put in a woodland glade or at the back of a large border.

Just one word of warning – you will have to be patient, for it takes time for the young tree to mature, and you might have to wait seven or eight years for the sensational bracts and fruits to appear.

JUNE: WEEK 2

Hosta fortunei
'Aureo-Marginata'

Thanks in part to American interest and breeding, hostas are infinitely varied in foliage and flower, very fashionable, and have their own appreciation society – the Hosta and Hemerocallis Society.

Garden Club visited a garden in Glasgow, whose owner specialized in hostas – she had collected at least two hundred different kinds and was still looking for new variations on the theme. Foliage ranged through colour – every gradation of green, from the electric bright gloss of *Hosta plantaginea*, to the dark blue green of *H. sieboldiana* 'Elegans' and there were wonderfully variegated leaves, like *Hosta fortunei* 'Albo-Picta' with bright yellow leaves edged with green, and *Hosta* 'Thomas Hogg', an old favourite, with white edging to dark green. Flowers too, were varied, from clear white to various shades of purple.

Roy Lancaster chose as his Plant of the Week *Hosta fortunei* 'Aureo-Marginata', which has green leaves with creamy-yellow margins, with lilac flowers in summer. Along with most of the variegated hostas, this one prefers shade, or at least partial shade, and moist, manure-enriched soil.

Once they are established, hostas keep down weeds very efficiently with their large

Hosta 'Blue Moon', nestling under the leaves of a rodgersia.

leaves. When they become too large, they can be propagated by lifting the plants in spring as the leaves are emerging and dividing them up into smaller clumps. I've seen this done, ruthlessly, with a spade, just as you would divide up a rhubarb crown, and slightly more delicately, with two garden hand forks, plunged back to back into the root system and gently forced apart.

Hostas always look best, in the smaller garden, when several different leaf forms are planted together. There were also some interesting combinations – hostas with ferns, hostas with old-fashioned roses, hostas with feathery plumed astilbes.

You have to be ruthless with the slugs, though, otherwise all will be lost. Most of the gardeners I spoke to defended their hostas with slug pellets, although there are other methods of warfare. (See Garden Horrors pp. 208).

JUNE: WEEK 3

Philadelphus 'Sybille'

The philadelphus has long been one of the most popular of our late spring or early summer shrubs. The 'Mock Orange', with its cloud of four-petalled white flowers and heady scent is familiar throughout the length and breadth of the country.

If you look through the catalogues, it may strike you that a high proportion of the names of our garden hybrids are French – 'Belle Etoile', 'Conquête', 'Bicolore', 'Etoile Rose', 'Girandole', 'Boule d'Argent' and the like. This is because many of them were raised by the hugely influential French firm of Lemoine, at the turn of the century.

Roy Lancaster recommended another of the Lemoine hybrids – *Philadelphus 'Sybille'*, dating originally from 1913. Its major merit is that it is comparatively small, growing to something about a metre by a metre across making it suitable for the smaller garden. The white flowers, on graceful, arching stems, are purple blotched at the throat, and have an interesting scent – not so much orange, more a tropical, banana-like aroma.

Like most of the members of its tribe, it will flourish and flower in poor soil, as long as it can see the sun. The species from which many of our garden hybrids are derived are *P. coronarius*, which grows on parched, rocky hillsides in Southern Austria and North and Central Italy and *P. microphyllus*, from canyons and woodlands in the Rocky Mountains of North America.

In cultivation in this country, the philadelphus hybrids need looking after – the stems which have flowered should be cut back, after flowering, to within two or three buds from the base. If it is abandoned, the plant can become a monster, producing huge shoots of bare wood, topped by foliage and a few flowers, searching for the sun. Even the obligingly small 'Sybille' will become a dull thing if it is not pruned regularly.

Propagation is by 10 cm cuttings from lateral shoots in July or August – the same time that you do the pruning. The cuttings should be rooted in peat and sand in a cold frame.

JUNE: WEEK 4

Genista aetnensis

Genistas, members of the broom family, come in all shapes and sizes. We have a tiny native broom, *Genista pilosa*, which grows to only a few centimetres high, and spreads across a rock garden, or by steps, to provide a golden carpet of flowers in May. At the other end of the scale, there is *Genista aetnensis*, which is the largest of them all, and can soar up to 6 metres and shows a mass of bright yellow, pea-like flowers growing from rush-like, almost leafless green stems, in July.

Roy Lancaster admired a splendid specimen of *Genista aetnensis*, of tree size, nestling next to a sunny wall in a garden in a Leicestershire village and pondered, as he so often does, the minor miracles of plant migration – this plant's natural home is on the ashy volcanic slopes of Mount Etna, in Sicily, (it is known as the Mount Etna Broom) and here it is growing and flowering quite happily in the middle of England.

Genista aetnensis is hardy and should do well anywhere in the country, provided it is given a sunny sheltered spot – and poor or sandy soil to remind it of home. It will need training to a single stem to reach this tree size and you should be careful, when pruning, not to cut into old wood, since it will not sprout again from such a cut. You should also decide, early on, where the plant is going to be allowed to flourish, for it does not like to be disturbed.

Propagation is by cuttings, taken in late summer. Being a species, it will come true from seed.

JULY: WEEK 1

Lavandula stoechas and *Lavandula stoechas pendunculata*

Life really can become most confusing when you go down to the garden centre these days and try to sort out the world of Lavenders. There's Old English Lavender, which could be listed as *L. angustifolia*, *L. officinalis* or *L. spica*, then there are dwarf lavenders, with English sounding names like 'Hidcote', 'Munstead' and 'Loddon Pink'. Dutch lavender, *L. vera*, may be on offer and over recent years, the so-called French lavender, *L. stoechas*, has become more popular.

L. stoechas looks quite different from the others. It has a cone, or flask, of tight flowers on each stem and on top of each cone, a tuft of purple bracts. The sub-species, *L.s. pendunculata*, may grow to 1 metre tall and its bracts are paler and larger. Both grow outdoors in the south, but in the north, it maybe wiser to grow them in pots, putting them outside in May and keeping a wary eye open for any late frosts.

All lavenders come from warm regions – many of them from the Mediterranean – and all of them thrive in their native regions in dry conditions, with very little in the way of food. They do well in this country, therefore, when they are planted in very chalky, sandy or gravelly soil. One expert has argued recently that we should be cruel to lavender, especially if it comes from the garden centre in a pot full of peat compost with a high fertilizer content – wash the stuff off, and plant your lavender in a sand, gravel and grit mix with some loam and a sprinkling of lime. It will need watering to get established, but should then be able to fend for itself just as it does in the *maquis* of Southern France or Corsica.

JULY: WEEK 2

Fremontodendron 'California Glory'

Fremontodendrons (still referred to by their old name of Fremontias in some reference books) are high-risk, high-reward, vigorous, high-growing shrubs, offering a long late spring to mid-summer season of lots of large, bold, buttery yellow flowers plus interesting evergreen foliage with a felty brown underside, rather like some rhododendrons.

The most successful have invariably been given support, usually up a south-facing wall or some sunny, sheltered position. Most are grown in the milder districts of Britain, in the south. The further north you see it flourishing, the more you must, respect the skills of the gardener who grows it. With tender loving care, it can reach 7 metres in less than ten years.

Fremontodendron 'California Glory' is a hybrid between Fremontodendron californicum,

discovered by John Charles Fremont, an officer in the US Corps of Topographical Engineers, in California in 1846, and Fremontodendron mexicanum, which comes from the Mexican side of the border. The cross was made in 1952 in Orange County, California, and was awarded a First Class Certificate by the RHS in 1967 and an Award of Garden Merit in 1984.

'California Glory' does well in poor soils – in fact if the soil is too rich, it will grow soft and be more susceptible to cold. If it gets too wet it can expire prematurely. If it becomes too straggly and untidy, it can be pruned back quite severely, but when you do that, make sure you wear gloves, safety goggles and a mask – those brown hairs on the underside of the leaves and other tiny hairs on some of the stems can cause irritation to the skin and more serious damage to lungs and eyes. Ravishing though it is, the fremontodendron is one of those plants which should really carry some sort of government health warning.

Opposite: **Lavandula stoechas pendunculata.**

JULY: WEEK 3

Lonicera tragophylla

Our native honeysuckle, *Lonicera peric-lymenum*, is a familiar and much-loved plant, scrambling, twining and climbing round hedgerows and even up trees, filling the air with intoxicating perfume as it flowers through the summer. Glistening red berries, in tight bunches, replace the flowers from August onwards. Its vernacular names are legion, a sure indication of its popularity – honeybind, trumpet flower, bugle bloom, evening pride and, of course, woodbine.

Lonicera tragophjylla is known as the Chinese woodbine and was introduced from that country at the turn of the century by E. H. Wilson. It is vigorous, deciduous, hardy and quite early on in the summer, produces large golden yellow flowers, like long heraldic trumpets. Later, after flowering, the scarlet fruits appear.

Almost any soil will do and an ideal situation would be somewhere where its roots can remain shady, cool and moist, while foliage and flower can bask in sunshine – having said that, it will also flower in a shady spot.

JULY: WEEK 4

Phlox maculata 'Omega'

The phlox is the hardy herbaceous perennial *par excellence*, providing clouds of colour, ranging through whites, lilacs, pinks, purples and reds, from July to September. Most are garden hybrids derived from the species *P. paniculata*.

P. maculata is not quite as well known, slightly smaller, sturdier, reaching 60 to 90 cm high, with a more limited range of colour, the flowers grouped in a cylindrical rather than a pyramidical shape at the head of the stem. Maculata means spotted and if you look, you can see maroon blotches on the stems. The variety which Roy Lancaster recommends is *P. maculata* 'Omega', which has white fragrant flowers with a lilac eye.

All phloxes are best planted in groups, with about 45 cm between each individual plant, in autumn or early spring. They should be well mulched in April and cut down after flowering to just above ground level. Eventually, when they are mature, they can be propagated by division in spring or autumn. They can also be increased by root cuttings, taken in winter. Keep the cuttings protected and moist and they should be ready for potting on or planting out the following May.

The dreaded enemy of the phlox is eel worm. If your plants are affected, the leaves will distort and discolour and turn into little more than twisted green threads. It is one of those afflictions for which there is no adequate cure. The only thing to do is to dig up the plants and burn them and make sure that you do not put phloxes back in that same spot for at least three years. Take heart though, the maculatas are less susceptible to eel worm than the paniculatas – and they should not need staking.

AUGUST: WEEK I

Calamintha nepeta

Calamintha comes from the Greek and, roughly translated, means 'beautiful mint' and there you have a perfect description of its scent.

It is a small plant, but, as Roy Lancaster likes to say, packs a big punch, reaching perhaps 45 cm in height, and being covered with lilac and white flowers from July right through to September or October – it has an extraordinarily long flowering season. Bees become positively ecstatic when the flowers are out and it is one of those plants which is nice to have somewhere by a path, so that you can easily reach it and crush the foliage in your fingers for the scent.

C. nepeta is an undemanding plant, easy to grow, thriving in ordinary soils somewhere in the sunshine. After a time, perhaps five years or more, it begins to lose its vigour, so it is a good idea to propagate new plants from the old. You can divide it in spring, or collect seed in late autumn and sow it in spring.

You can find Calamintha nepeta growing wild in Britain, usually on chalky soils, in locations as far apart as Kent, Yorkshire and Pembroke. Its territory is wide – it also grows in southern Europe and by the Mediterranean. Roy Lancaster has seen it flourishing in the sunshine of Tuscany, springing from ancient Etruscan tombstones.

Calamintha nepeta is one of those confusing plants which is listed under different names in the catalogues – sometimes as Calamintha nepetoides, sometimes as Satureja calamintha.

AUGUST: WEEK 2

Crocosmia
'Star of the East'

The common montbretia is a tough old ruffian from South Africa – a perennial which grows from corms, and has long green sword-shaped leaves and flowers which are various shades of orange. It is almost indestructible, surviving in abandoned gardens and even surging up into flower when it has been thrown away on rubbish heaps and tips.

The garden hybrid crocosmias are closely related, but much more aristocratic cousins. Alan Bloom has introduced some vigorous new members of the family from his world-famous nursery at Bressingham, in Norfolk. Crocosmia 'Lucifer', as its name suggests, is a blazing red, while C. 'Spitfire' has reddish-orange blooms. Roy Lancaster delved further back into the history of another famous garden when he chose Crocosmia 'Star of the East' as his plant of the week. It was first found, in 1912, at Hidcote Manor, in the Cotswolds in Gloucestershire, a garden which in its time shaped and changed the history of gardening in Britain.

C. 'Star of the East' grows to about one metre, with apricot, star-like flowers in late summer. It does best in sandy well-drained soils and must be able to see plenty of sunshine. If it is happy, it will increase.

Spiraea japonica 'Anthony Waterer'

Our great-grandfathers knew, loved and grew *Spiraea japonica* 'Anthony Waterer': it has been a popular garden shrub since it was first introduced into commerce well over a hundred years ago, after appearing as a sport in Anthony Waterer's nursery at Knap Hill, in Surrey, in the 1870s.

It will grow almost anywhere as long as it gets some sun, producing fluffy pink flower heads in late summer, over deciduous foliage which can sometimes be green, sometimes variegated with cream and green. You should prune out weak shoots and cut back longer healthier ones in February or March on an established shrub, otherwise it can get straggly, untidy and tired-looking. Some brave souls cut back the whole thing occasionally.

Spiraea japonica 'Goldflame' is a modern variety, slightly smaller, growing perhaps 80 cm tall. There are the usual pink flowers in summer, but the foliage is a rich, burned orange-brown, turning yellow and then green in autumn.

An even smaller variety, suitable for a large rock garden, is *Spiraea japonica* 'Golden Princess', which as the name suggests, has golden green foliage beneath the pink flowers. This one should not get more than 30 to 60 cm high.

Lastly, for the gardener who may already be familiar with all the varieties mentioned so far, Roy Lancaster suggests a curiosity, only recently introduced into this country, *Spiraea japonica* 'Shiburi' sometimes known, incorrectly as 'Shirobana', which delivers pink *and* white flowers above green foliage. With this one, we are back to the same sort of height and spread you would expect with Anthony Waterer, some 60 to 90 cm tall and the same across.

Buddleia davidii 'Dartmoor'

It is hard to believe that *Buddleia davidii* is not a native British plant, for you find it growing, not just in gardens, but apparently wild in all sorts of wayside places. We all call it the Butterfly Bush, because it attracts clouds of butterflies when it flowers lilac or purple plumes in July and that makes it sound even more homely.

This buddleia comes, in fact, from the other side of the world: it was first discovered by another of those French missionary/plant hunters, Armand David, in 1869. The major introduction to this country came from seed collected by E. H. Wilson around the turn of the century. He called it his Summer Lilac: it has become a popular garden shrub. The buddleia, then, was a garden plant which jumped over the wall and spread by parachuting its seed everywhere.

Buddleia davidii 'Dartmoor' was, in effect, a wild plant, recaptured for the garden. It was found by a Mr Hayles, while he was on holiday in Devon, in 1971. He noted its large panicles of rich magenta flowers, took some cuttings, brought them home and succeeded in rooting them. Two years later, 'Dartmoor' won the RHS Award of Merit.

B.d. 'Dartmoor', like most of its kind, will grow in poor soils, acid or alkaline. You can prune the shoots which have flowered the previous summer, in late winter or early spring, right back to within a bud or two from the ground and it will shoot up even more vigorously. Propagation is by cuttings in summer – which was just what Mr Hayles did. It might be interesting to collect seed, although there is no telling what you might end up with.

Sedum 'Vera Jameson'.

SEPTEMBER: WEEK 1

Sedums for the autumn border

The sedums are a family of succulent plants – many of them are quite small and at home in hot rocky places and on walls, hence their common name of stonecrops. There are some larger members of the group, however, which are grown as hardy perennials in the herbaceous border, where they tend to come into their own in autumn.

The best known of these, much beloved by garden centres, is probably *Sedum spectabile* 'Autumn Joy', which grows up to 60 cm tall and has large heads, a bit like cauliflower curds, made up of hundreds of tiny star-shaped flowers, pink at first, then deepening to a rusty red. Bees and butterflies love it, as they do all the herbaceous border sedums.

Roy Lancaster chose three slightly more unusual, autumn-flowering sedums. The first, *Sedum maximum* 'Atropurpureum', has dark purple stems and, in September and October, rose-red flowers. It has a somewhat gawky habit, reaching 60 cm in height – it may need some sort of unobtrusive support.

Sedum 'Ruby Glow' is a smaller, floppier plant, with rosy stems, leaves and flowers. It is better grown in a raised bed, where it can drape itself gracefully over the edge, but you can put it at the front of the border where you might have to manoeuvre round it with the lawn mower.

Sedum 'Vera Jameson' is a hybrid between the two which emerged as a seedling in the late Mrs Jameson's garden in Gloucestershire and, as you might expect, it is half way between the first two in size, having purple foliage and deep pink flowers.

All sedums look even more impressive when two or three are planted together. You could buy one plant to begin with, then, when it has matured, propagate by dividing it, or by root cuttings in either spring or summer.

Perovskia atriplicifolia 'Blue Spire'

There is a lovely example of *Perovskia atriplicifolia* 'Blue Spire' just outside the RHS garden at Wisley, planted in a raised, brick-sided bed. The tall stems look white and closer examination reveals that they are covered with a whitish, grey powdery down, while the grey-green leaves are aromatic and remind me of the smell of sage. In late August and early September it is covered in small two-lipped deep violet flowers. The plant itself reaches some 120–150 cm and the raised bed makes it look even taller.

The original home of *Perovskia atriplicifolia* is in the Western Himalayas, Afghanistan and Tibet, where it grows in harsh dry conditions along the stony slopes of valleys – it does well in Britain in poor sandy soils and even on chalk, as long as it is in a sunny and well-drained spot.

It is a sub-shrub, which means that it has a perennial woody framework which produces softish herbaceous growth likely to die back in winter – it is advisable to cut down the stem quite low in early spring, to encourage new strong growth each year. The RHS example is not supported, but some gardeners do play safe and support the stems with canes. Roy Lancaster suggests that if you buy a long-stemmed plant from a garden centre, it probably makes sense to protect the stems by tying them to a cane, at least until you get it home, because the stems are easily broken.

Mr Perovsky was the governor of a remote Russian province in the early nineteenth century and the plant named after him came to Britain in 1904, although precious little is known about that. 'Blue Spire', which is a selection from the species, arrived in this country from a German nursery – at that time it was called, with Teutonic taxonomical accuracy *Perovskia atriplicifolia erecta*. Notcutts, the famous Woodbridge nursery, distributed it in Britain and someone there came up with the romantic (but still accurate) name 'Blue Spire'.

Cuttings can be taken, of semi-ripe wood, in July or August. The original plant eventually gets too woody, and this is the way to renew it.

SEPTEMBER: WEEK 3

Cotinus
'Grace'

The deciduous shrub *Cotinus* 'Grace' is a comparative newcomer to the garden scene and its recent history and development can be accurately charted.

Cotinus coggygria, the Venetian sumach, has been with us a long time and is a familiar plant in many gardens. It has fluffy clouds of delicate pink flowers in June and July. Eventually, the pink turns to grey and when that happens, you can perfectly understand how it acquired the popular name of the Smoke bush, or Smoke tree, for the flowers now look like wreaths and wisps of smoke around the rounded bulk of reddish-purple leaves. In autumn, those leaves turn a startling fiery red. Roy Lancaster has seen acres of it planted on the hills above the Great Wall of China and describes how the whole landscape seems ablaze.

On the other side of the world, in North America, the only other member of the genus, *Cotinus obovatus*, is native to Tennessee, Alabama and Texas, where it is known as the Chittamwood, or American Smoke tree. It has larger leaves and flowers than *C. coggygria*.

As recently as 1977, the two were brought together by Peter Dummer, the Master Propagator at Hillier's Nurseries, in Hampshire. Mr Dummer crossed the American plant with 'Velvet Cloak', a purple-based form of the other, to produce his hybrid, which he named after his wife. The hybrid has leaves which are wine-red when young, mature to a rich plum and expire in autumn in a fiery red. The flower heads are pink, and very large.

The plant has a distinguished history – an Award of Merit and the Reginald Cory Cup, the latter given by the RHS to the best deliberate garden hybrid of the year, in 1983, and the accolade of a First Class Certificate in 1990.

Cotinus 'Grace' is not fussy about acid or alkaline soils, nor does it need a rich soil. Give it a well-drained sunny spot and it should thrive. Roy Lancaster estimates that it may eventually get up to 6 metres high, if it is content, although it may be hard pruned in late winter to keep it more manageable.

Ceratostigma willmottianum

Ceratostigma willmottianum is a small, half-hardy shrub, with unusual diamond-shaped dark green leaves which can turn red in autumn. The flowers bloom in late summer and sometimes through until autumn – they are a striking deep blue.

A sheltered and sunny south-facing border is the place to put it. You will need to protect it during the winter – after a series of hard frosts, it may die right down to the ground, but the roots should survive to put up new roots in the spring. In recent years, the winters have not been at all harsh and the plant has survived almost intact in many areas.

All the same, it is probably a good idea to propagate. The safest thing to do is to take long heel cuttings, in July. Root them in a warm place, in a mixture of peat and sand, then transfer them to pots of John Innes Number 1 compost. They can go out in a cold frame until the following spring.

Ceratostigma willmottianum is yet another plant from the vast treasury introduced by E. H. Wilson from China. This one was found high up on the mountainsides above the valley of the river Min, in Western Sichuan, in 1908. Only two of Wilson's seeds germinated and it is said that all the plants in the country derive from those two seedlings. There's a challenge for you – see if you can propagate your own plant from seed!

Pyracantha 'Orange Glow'

It is hard to believe, when you buy a metre-high pyracantha, or firethorn, taped to a cane in a modest plastic pot, that you are investing in something which could eventually cover the side of a house. It is an evergreen, and against the permanent background of green, there are two startling seasonal performances – in spring, it is smothered with white blossom, while in autumn there is a dazzling display of red, orange or yellow berries which can last right through until the following March.

If you do choose to plant your pyracanthas by a wall, or fence, it will need some form of support to help it climb – usually horizontal wires. Any shoots which rebel from this discipline and grow outwards should be pruned out or, better, looped back, for you can overdo the pruning and deprive yourself of both flower and fruit.

You can, of course, raise a pyracantha as a shrub, or use it as a hedging plant, although the same warnings about over-enthusiastic pruning would apply.

From the dozens of pyracanthas available, Roy Lancaster recommends *Pyracantha* 'Orange Glow', a plant first raised in Holland in the 1930s and brought into commerce twenty years later, plus two German-bred varieties – 'Orange Charmer', which, not surprisingly, has orange berries and 'Golden Charmer', which has yellow berries. 'Saphyr Orange' and 'Saphyr Rouge', with orange and red berries respectively, are recently introduced French firethorns, bred for their resistance to disease.

A pyracantha grown as a standard in Welwyn.

OCTOBER: WEEK 2

Elaeagnus x ebbingei 'Gilt Edge'

Elaeagnus x ebbingei 'Gilt Edge' is an evergreen shrub, with leathery, shiny green leaves whose edges look as if they have been dipped and splashed, somewhat clumsily, in yellow-gold paint. The undersides of the leaves are silvery. In autumn, there are small, creamy white scented flowers tucked away secretively in the axils of the leaves – they are followed by modest red fruits.

A tough customer, it will do well in most soils and in most parts of Britain, although it may take time to settle in colder areas. It is one of those plants especially useful in seaside locations, since it is reasonably tolerant of salt spray breezes. Eventually, it should become a slightly untidy globe, about 2–3 metres across.

'Gilt Edge' is a sport, found in a British nursery in 1966, on a plain grey-green leaved *Elaeagnus x ebbingei*, itself a hybrid of the Japanese species *Elaeagnus pungens*. Like many such creatures, it may revert, throwing up a shoot of green leaves in the midst of all the variegation. If that happens, the greenery must be pruned out.

Flower arrangers love 'Gilt Edge' and may be tempted to plunder it too much at one go. This overharvesting can encourage reversion. Propagation is by cuttings in summer or autumn.

OCTOBER: WEEK 3

Amelanchier lamarckii

There is a hedge of *Amelanchier lamarckii* in a raised bed next door to the Granada Television Studios in Manchester. I used to work there and I enjoyed marking off the seasons as the hedge flowered in spring, then berried and unfolded magnificent autumn colour. Finally, I thought it would be nice to have a single specimen in my garden at home.

I've gradually pruned away stems until it now grows on a single stem, as a small tree. Roy Lancaster says it could get up to 8 metres eventually, but at the moment it seems to be sitting comfortably at about half that, after some ten years.

Amelanchier lamarckii comes originally from North America, and is thought to have arrived in this country in the early nineteenth century. Strangely, it is no longer to be found in the wild in its native country, but can be seen growing wild across the Southern Counties from Kent to Dorset, the theory being that these plants were sown by birds who had feasted on the berries of a tree in a domestic garden, then deposited the seeds. It seems to thrive on poor, acid, sandy soils.

The shrub, or tree, is sometimes commonly called the Snowy Mespilus, a name which refers to the wonderful cascade of bright white starry flowers which it produces briefly in late April. The young foliage unfurling at the same time is a lovely soft coppery-pink. Later, green berries arrive – they turn red, then finally black in mid-summer. They tell me that you can eat the berries, preferably in a pie. In autumn, the leaves glow with a pyrotechnic display through yellow, orange and bright scarlet before they fall in late October. *Amelanchier lamarckii* 'Ballerina' is more free fruiting, although its autumn tints are darker.

OCTOBER: WEEK 4

Nerine bowdenii

Nerine bowdenii comes from South Africa, where it was first found among screes and ledges at the foot of the Drakensberg Mountains. It is a welcome introduction and brings a warm splash of colour to the garden in September, October and into November, with six-petalled bright pink flowers which look as if they have been peeled back from some exotic fruit. It can reach up to 80 cm in height.

Bulbs are usually planted in late summer, in a border in a warm, sunny position – a favourite spot seems to be the south side of a greenhouse or shed. They should be planted quite shallowly, so their tips are just above the surface of the soil – the notion being that they like to be baked by the sun. One gardener I met said that he always watered his bulbs regularly from July onwards, as they were getting ready to flower, and that seemed to do them a lot of good.

There is a variety of the plant called 'Mark Fenwick', or 'Fenwick's Variety', which is taller and more vigorous than the species and has flowers of a deeper pink. Mark Fenwick was the owner of what was, in the 1930s, one of the great gardens of Britain – Abbotswood, near Stow in the Wold, in Gloucestershire. The 'new' nerine was found flowering there in the garden. In 1945, *Nerine bowdenii* 'Fenwick's Variety' received an Award of Merit at the Royal Horticultural Society's Great Autumn Show. Over twenty years later, in 1966, it gained a First Class Certificate, and is now called *N. bowdenii* 'Mark Fenwick'.

Garden horrors

The roll call of things that can go wrong in the garden is endless. During the course of a year with the *Garden Club* gardeners, I heard chilling tales of chrysanthemums wiped out by white rust, phlox devastated by eelworm, tulips ruined by tulip fire, flowering cherries debilitated by bacterial canker and gardens overrun by rampant and apparently unstoppable weeds, among many other tales of woe. Everything turned out all right in the end, of course, because keen gardeners are a resilient breed, and usually find ways round the problems.

I've picked out half a dozen horrors which crop up time and time again in gardens all over the country and tried to show the various ways *Garden Club* members tackled them, often without resorting to chemical warfare.

Opposite: **Japanese knotweed poised for an attack on a Swansea garden.**

Slugs and snails

There are very few gardens without slugs, although I did come across one happy gardener by the Humber who claimed that they did not bother him too much – his soil was mostly sharp sand. Most though, have experienced the devastation wreaked by these creatures – lettuce shredded, hostas in tatters, runner beans nipped off before they can run, strawberries ruined. The first reaction is to reach for the slug pellets and let them have it.

A substantial proportion of *Garden Club* members are not as keen on slug pellets as they used to be. As it tells you quite clearly on the packet, the pellets are poisonous and the poisons may be passed on up the food chain, via the creatures who choose to feed on those awful slimy corpses – and they could include thrushes, or even dogs. So the reformed gardeners have tried a variety of preventative methods.

The theory that slugs do not like to drag their feet, or rather their soft underbellies, over abrasive matter is well founded – hence the happiness of the Humberside gardener. A retired market gardener in Shrewsbury reckons that a ring of soot, flue-dust, sharp sand or baked, crushed eggshells will protect tender young plants, although that protective ring can be broken by heavy rain – and slugs can be very active after heavy rain.

A wildlife enthusiast in Norwich, who would not hurt a fly, let along a slug, goes out at night with a torch and picks up the offenders by hand although, come to think of it, she did not tell me what she did with them after that. The same lady deals with slugs in the greenhouse by leaving half a scooped out orange or lemon, cut side down, with an entrance cut in it, like a little citrus igloo, on the floor. The slugs congregate there overnight and can be disposed of in the morning. Outdoors, she encourages natural predators, such as thrushes and toads, by providing them with an environment they like and they help to keep down the slugs.

The beer trap offers an interesting method of defence: a saucer is sunk level with the soil, then filled to brim with beer. Slugs sip the amber nectar, become more enthusiastic for the stuff, fall into the saucer and drown.

Apparently there has been research in America which shows that different slugs like different sorts of beer – some like real ale, others prefer lager. (I am not making this up but quote Alan Gear, the chief executive of the Henry Doubleday Research Association, no less.) The HDA is also working on a research project which suggests that it might be useful to introduce another predator into sensitive parts of the garden – *Abax paral lelepidus*, a ferocious beetle with a taste for slugs.

Honey Fungus

I remember one spring day, walking round a garden in South Wales with Roy Lancaster and the proud owners of the garden, a few days prior to filming a piece for Garden Club. The owners had every right to be proud – their garden, thirty-five years in the making, was large and wholly delightful, swooping down a valley to a stream and richly stocked with shrubs and lovely mature specimen trees. As Roy congratulated them on what they had achieved, the lady said, almost as a joke, that she hoped they never got honey fungus. Roy replied casually that it was probably already there, somewhere, since many gardens have it. The lady was thunderstruck and started looking nervously around, as if some nightmare had begun to happen.

Armillaria mellea, or bootlace fungus, shoestring fungus, collar rot fungus or honey fungus, as it is variously and colloquially called *is* a nightmare and can destroy trees, shrubs and other garden plants before you are even aware that it is there. The fungus lives on rotting wood, such as old tree stumps and sometimes (but not always) sends out underground rhizomorphs, which look like black or brown bootlaces and travel underground to search for further food supplies. Those rhizomorphs can penetrate living roots of other plants and eventually kill them, spreading a white, fan-shaped sheet under the bark. A wet, white rot can sometimes be found round the collar of the tree or shrub. In some seasons (but not necessarily every year), the fungus fruits in autumn and puts up toadstools whose caps look as if they have been drenched in shiny golden honey.

Once the fungus is detected, by far and away the best thing to do is ruthlessly to get rid of the infected plant and burn it. One *Garden Club* member had the fungus infect just one plant in a hedge of privet, but had wisely ripped up and destroyed other plants within several feet of the dead one. At the RHS garden at Wisley, they removed a double avenue of whitebeams when they found that a few were infected. You can also dig up the soil around a plant you have removed, and soak the ground with a phenolic emulsion, called Armillatox, which should kill off the rhizomorphs.

Keep your fingers crossed – honey fungus probably is in your garden, but it may stay there harmlessly feeding on dead material without ever turning nasty.

Ground Elder

Ground elder, (*Aegopodium podagraria*) also known in some quarters as Bishop's Weed, or Goutweed, is a perennial weed of quite extraordinary persistence. You will recognize it by its hollow, fluted stems, which look a bit like thin celery, and its bright green saw-edged leaves – it spreads by white rhizomes, which can be creeping about, unseen, for yards all around the plant. The flowers, which arrive in June or July, are white, on umbrella-shaped stalks.

One way of getting rid of ground elder is to smother it completely in spring, covering it with a thick mulch of grass cuttings, leaves, sawdust or thick black polythene. You inspect from time to time through the year, turning the mulch, picking out and destroying any ground elder which has survived, and re-cover. It takes a long time, it isn't pretty and it kills everything else under the blanket, but it is a fairly effective way of eradicating the beast.

If you find ground elder lurking among your perennial beds, or in the rockery, then the best thing to do is lift all the plants you want to keep and put them in uncontaminated soil somewhere else in the garden, while you tackle the offending weed by hand, pulling out every fragment of it, waiting a few weeks, then pulling out everything that reappears.

The worst scenario occurs when ground elder gets in among established trees and shrubs, which cannot be moved. Now you must revert to chemical control, which must, of course, be done very carefully. Glyphosate acts on foliage and is then translocated to other parts of the plant. If you use it in the form of a spray, then you must mask off any other foliage that may be at risk in the area, and you should always spray on a calm day. If you use it as a gel, then just the offending leaves are treated. You may have to treat more than once.

It was called Goutweed, by the way, because a poultice made from the boiled leaves and roots of the plant was supposed to help those suffering from gout.

Clubroot

Clubroot disease is the scourge of brassicas – cabbages, cauliflowers, sprouts and the like – and some gardeners simply give up trying to grow these kinds of vegetables once the scourge has struck. Professional growers who have been hit by the disease have been known to abandon the infected ground and move operations elsewhere.

The cause of the disease is an organism called *Plasmodiophora brassicae*, which swarms in the soil in the form of tiny spores. The National Vegetable Research Station has calculated that there could be up to 100,000 million spores under each square metre of soil when the bug is active – and they can survive for up to twenty years, patiently waiting until a susceptible plant is put their way.

The spores germinate into something called a swimming swarm spore, and penetrate the root system of the victim. When this happens, the root distorts and swells into something that looks like a parrot's swollen claw – 'clubroot'. The plant dies, of course.

Amateurs are advised to concentrate on prevention, for a cure can be very expensive and involves using dangerous chemicals. For reasons which are not yet clear, clubroot does not thrive in alkaline soil – the NVRS says that a pH of about 7 is probably the most useful for clubroot suppression. Well-drained, light soils don't seem to be badly affected. It is probably safer to raise your own brassicas from seed, rather than buy plants. Finally, never borrow garden tools from anyone who has the disease in his garden – and if you visit an infested garden, scrub your boots with hot soapy water immediately afterwards.

Japanese Knotweed

I had seen Japanese knotweed before, of course, usually by rivers and streams in abandoned industrial areas of the north–west of Britain, where its bamboo-like jointed hollow stalks, with huge heart-shaped leaves and long feathery clusters of flowers dangling from each node in summer and into autumn look odd, exotic, romantic even. It was introduced into this country about a hundred and fifty years ago, from Japan, as a garden ornamental; it leapt the garden wall, as so many of these plants did, and now leads a formidable life of its own, reaching ten feet and more in height and forming large clumps where nothing much else can survive. When it tries to get back into the garden – your garden – you are in trouble.

Japanese knotweed *Reynoutria japonica* (*Polygonum cuspidatum*) spreads vegetatively underground. It does produce seed, and seedlings, but, oddly enough, they seem to die off. The recommended cure is to use a translocated chemical, such as Glyphosate, sprayed on, with the usual precautions, when the foliage of the plant is well developed in late spring or early summer.

In the case of the garden we saw in South Wales, with a huge embankment at the side of the house full of Japanese knotweed, this treatment simply hadn't worked. The embankment was grassed over and daffodils planted – when they finished flowering each year, the knotweed was just coming up, for all the world like a bizarre rhubarb. The owner had found that the only thing to do was to strim down everything, and keep on strimming at least once a week, in the hope that the weed would give up and go away.

Vine Weevil

The trade mark of the adult vine weevil beetle is a series of notches – someone once described them to me as looking like the holes bus conductors used to punch the edge of tickets – chewed from the margins of leaves, usually leaves on lower branches of plants and shrubs. The creature is known to have an appetite for *Euonymous fortunei*, azaleas, rhododendrons and camellias.

The culprits are small black beetles, with brown patches on their wing cases which make them look faintly speckled, and curious jointed, or elbowed antennae. They spend the day dozing in dark places and only move about at night – they can't fly, but walk everywhere and can climb, in a very slow, but very determined fashion and to places you might have thought were inaccessible.

It is possible to control them with spraying or dusting with chemicals and there are several proprietary brands on offer. Most of the *Garden Club* members I met don't like using such methods and instead go out at night with a torch and pick them off by hand, or put a newspaper under the shrub and shake the branches so the beetles fall out on the paper. I draw a veil over what happens next, but heavy garden boots are useful.

Vine weevil grubs can cause havoc in pot plants in the greenhouse, in containers outside, or in the garden itself. They go for lots of favourite plants, like fuchsias, saintpaulias, begonias, pelargoniums, impatiens, coleus, sedums and cyclamen. They eat roots and burrow into corms and the first sign you are likely to see is an unrescuable collapsed plant. If you sift through the compost, you will find them – little white, plump grubs with pale brown heads. One gardener I know throws the compost on his lawn and much enjoys the sight of the birds feasting on the grubs.

Again, they can be controlled by using chemicals such as permethrin, HCH, or pirimiphos-methyl, but if you don't like the idea of that, there are methods of biological control in the greenhouse, using nematodes, which burrow into the grubs and kill them, feeding on the bacteria of the corpses. The nematodes, microscopic thread-like worms, packed by the million into a solution absorbed into a sponge, can be bought, squeezed out into water and applied as a drench. They only function in soil temperatures of 10–21°C, so are not likely to be effective outside.

Photograph Acknowledgements

All photographs taken by Stephen Robson with the exception of the following:

Steward Sadd of Channel Four: p. ii, vi, 3, 9, 10, 166, 178, 185.
Richard Alty: p. 16/17, 65, 177, 189.
Roy Lancaster: p. 181, 183, 187, 188, 190, 194, 195, 199, 201, 204.
Garden Picture Library: p. 41, (Clive Nichols), 42, 70 (John Glover), 45 (Joanne Pavia), 57 (John Neubauer), 60 (Clay Perry), 75 (Henk Dijkman), 108 (J. S. Sira), 133 (Jerry Pavia), 160/1 (Stephen Wooster).

Index